OPPOSING
VIEWPOINTS®
SERIES

✓ S0-DUT-608

| Capitalism

Other Books of Related Interest

Opposing Viewpoints Series

The Corporatization of America
Poverty, Prosperity, and the Minimum Wage
White Collar Crime

At Issue Series

Is America a Democracy or an Oligarchy?
Political Corruption
Student Debt

Current Controversies Series

Fair Trade
The Gig Economy
Libertarians, Socialists, and Other Third Parties

> "Congress shall make no law ... abridging the freedom of speech, or of the press."

First Amendment to the U.S. Constitution

The basic foundation of our democracy is the First Amendment guarantee of freedom of expression. The Opposing Viewpoints series is dedicated to the concept of this basic freedom and the idea that it is more important to practice it than to enshrine it.

OPPOSING
VIEWPOINTS®
SERIES

| Capitalism

Andrew Karpan, Book Editor

GREENHAVEN
PUBLISHING

Published in 2023 by Greenhaven Publishing, LLC
2544 Clinton Street,
Buffalo NY 14224

Articles in Greenhaven Publishing anthologies are often edited for length to meet page
requirements. In addition, original titles of these works are changed to clearly present
the main thesis and to explicitly indicate the author's opinion. Every effort is made to
ensure that Greenhaven Publishing accurately reflects the original intent of the authors.
Every effort has been made to trace the owners of the copyrighted material.

Cover image: 89stocker/Shutterstock.com

Library of Congress CataloginginPublication Data

Names: Karpan, Andrew, editor.
Title: Capitalism / Andrew Karpan, book editor.
Description: First Edition. | Buffalo, NY : Greenhaven Publishing, [2024] |
    Series: Opposing viewpoints | Includes bibliographical references and
    index. | Audience: Grades 10-12
Identifiers: LCCN 2023005348 | ISBN 9781534509474 (library binding) | ISBN
    9781534509467 (paperback)
Subjects: LCSH: Capitalism--Juvenile literature. | Economic
    policy--Juvenile literature.
Classification: LCC HB501 .C242247 2024 | DDC 306.3/42--dc23/eng/20230313
LC record available at https://lccn.loc.gov/2023005348

Manufactured in the United States of America

Website: http://greenhavenpublishing.com

Contents

Chapter 3: Are There Any Modern Alternatives to Capitalism?

Chapter 4: Is Capitalism a Force for Moral Good?

The Importance of Opposing Viewpoints

Perhaps every generation experiences a period in time in which the populace seems especially polarized, starkly divided on the important issues of the day and gravitating toward the far ends of the political spectrum and away from a consensus-facilitating middle ground. The world that today's students are growing up in and that they will soon enter into as active and engaged citizens is deeply fragmented in just this way. Issues relating to terrorism, immigration, women's rights, minority rights, race relations, health care, taxation, wealth and poverty, the environment, policing, military intervention, the proper role of government—in some ways, perennial issues that are freshly and uniquely urgent and vital with each new generation—are currently roiling the world.

If we are to foster a knowledgeable, responsible, active, and engaged citizenry among today's youth, we must provide them with the intellectual, interpretive, and critical-thinking tools and experience necessary to make sense of the world around them and of the all-important debates and arguments that inform it. After all, the outcome of these debates will in large measure determine the future course, prospects, and outcomes of the world and its peoples, particularly its youth. If they are to become successful members of society and productive and informed citizens, students need to learn how to evaluate the strengths and weaknesses of someone else's arguments, how to sift fact from opinion and fallacy, and how to test the relative merits and validity of their own opinions against the known facts and the best possible available information. The landmark series Opposing Viewpoints has been providing students with just such critical-thinking skills and exposure to the debates surrounding society's most urgent contemporary issues for many years, and it continues to serve this essential role with undiminished commitment, care, and rigor.

The key to the series's success in achieving its goal of sharpening students' critical-thinking and analytic skills resides in its title—

Opposing Viewpoints. In every intriguing, compelling, and engaging volume of this series, readers are presented with the widest possible spectrum of distinct viewpoints, expert opinions, and informed argumentation and commentary, supplied by some of today's leading academics, thinkers, analysts, politicians, policy makers, economists, activists, change agents, and advocates. Every opinion and argument anthologized here is presented objectively and accorded respect. There is no editorializing in any introductory text or in the arrangement and order of the pieces. No piece is included as a "straw man," an easy ideological target for cheap point-scoring. As wide and inclusive a range of viewpoints as possible is offered, with no privileging of one particular political ideology or cultural perspective over another. It is left to each individual reader to evaluate the relative merits of each argument—as he or she sees it, and with the use of ever-growing critical-thinking skills—and grapple with his or her own assumptions, beliefs, and perspectives to determine how convincing or successful any given argument is and how the reader's own stance on the issue may be modified or altered in response to it.

This process is facilitated and supported by volume, chapter, and selection introductions that provide readers with the essential context they need to begin engaging with the spotlighted issues, with the debates surrounding them, and with their own perhaps shifting or nascent opinions on them. In addition, guided reading and discussion questions encourage readers to determine the authors' point of view and purpose, interrogate and analyze the various arguments and their rhetoric and structure, evaluate the arguments' strengths and weaknesses, test their claims against available facts and evidence, judge the validity of the reasoning, and bring into clearer, sharper focus the reader's own beliefs and conclusions and how they may differ from or align with those in the collection or those of their classmates.

Research has shown that reading comprehension skills improve dramatically when students are provided with compelling, intriguing, and relevant "discussable" texts. The subject matter of these collections could not be more compelling, intriguing, or urgently relevant to today's students and the world they are poised to inherit. The anthologized articles and the reading and discussion questions that are included with them also provide the basis for stimulating, lively, and passionate classroom debates. Students who are compelled to anticipate objections to their own argument and identify the flaws in those of an opponent read more carefully, think more critically, and steep themselves in relevant context, facts, and information more thoroughly. In short, using discussable text of the kind provided by every single volume in the Opposing Viewpoints series encourages close reading, facilitates reading comprehension, fosters research, strengthens critical thinking, and greatly enlivens and energizes classroom discussion and participation. The entire learning process is deepened, extended, and strengthened.

For all of these reasons, Opposing Viewpoints continues to be exactly the right resource at exactly the right time—when we most need to provide readers with the critical-thinking tools and skills that will not only serve them well in school but also in their careers and their daily lives as decision-making family members, community members, and citizens. This series encourages respectful engagement with and analysis of opposing viewpoints and fosters a resulting increase in the strength and rigor of one's own opinions and stances. As such, it helps make readers "future ready," and that readiness will pay rich dividends for the readers themselves, for the citizenry, for our society, and for the world at large.

Introduction

> *"Capitalism does not require us to hold a particular set of cognitive beliefs; it only requires that we act as if certain beliefs (about money, commodities, etc.) are true. The rituals are the beliefs, beliefs which, at the level of subjective self-description, may well be disavowed."*
>
> —*Mark Fisher, English cultural and political theorist*

For most of the last two hundred years, there have been people waiting for the fall of capitalism. Nevertheless, it remains, persisting after every economic downturn as a force stronger than it's ever been before. The banks that finance it may crash, and the businesses that extol its virtues may eventually flop belly-up, but nevertheless it persists. The system churns on, forgetting the mistakes of history and remembering only its triumphs. Endemic to the language of capitalism is success; the business of getting bigger and richer.

But these successes are not without their critics. If the system failed to fall of its own accord, did not quite collapse onto the ash heap of history like everything else since the age of the robber barons, then it was still not very great, regardless of its remarkable capacity for persisting. They argue that under capitalism, resources are distributed unevenly, and some people are left without enough for survival. Environmental catastrophe is fueled by greed inherent to the system. Even if capitalism continues to function as an economic system, some argue that it is incompatible with a sustainable social system.

The chapters in this book survey these arguments from capitalism's detractors as well as pro-capitalist voices, which remain a loud constituency in just about every country in the world. Those in support of capitalism argue that it is the natural economic order. In fact, some adherents to this worldview are of the opinion that capitalism is, itself, a kind of unrestrained version of human nature. Capitalism is the language of the marketplace, which has persisted since the era of early agriculture. Other supporters suggest that inequality is not an inherent aspect of the system—that anyone with talent who puts in enough hard work has a chance for success.

However, detractors argue that capitalism has fueled many of the great evils of history. Systems of oppression, like slavery, expanded around the world as just another money-making opportunity, and the long fight against the corresponding legacy of racial oppression has long attracted anti-capitalist revolutionaries. In the past century, those revolutionaries have taken the form of Soviet communists, and they've taken the form of modest social democrats who run in elections and suggest nationalizing key utilities.

It's perhaps this tension between those who believe capitalism helps maintain society and those who believe it simply fuels humanity's worst instincts that explains why capitalism is always, especially now, in a moment of crisis. The latest event has shaken the walls in ways they have never shook before. This has taken the form of the implosion of the housing market in 2008. The extended occupation of a public park near Wall Street by unhappy protesters. The 2016 election of Donald Trump, a popular symbol of capitalism, as president of the world's biggest capitalist nation. The COVID-19 pandemic, which suddenly shut down economic infrastructure, causing food to rot in the fields, people to lose their livelihoods, supply chains to be disrupted, and bodies to pile up in hospitals. How would capitalism get out of this one?

Supporters of capitalism say that the system survives these challenges, in part, because of the moral goodness that the system creates. Accompanying the economy of buying has always been the economy of giving known as philanthropism. Excess capital, like furniture bought for a different apartment, is voluntarily distributed through the rungs of society in exchange for power or prestige. The pundits say that nobody else gives quite like Americans. The gesture of giving is a fundamental part of the culture, the country's mythology full of affluent individuals who choose to give back to their communities.

But critics are suspicious of the concept of philanthropy too. The money that is being given disappears with its act of kindness. These "philanthropic" donations often experience little scrutiny or regulation. The so-called "nonprofit" is a tax term and carries very little intrinsic meaning. So-called "political" nonprofits become ways of moving money from the wealthy and into the pockets of the powerful, whose political campaigns become "charitable" causes for their donation.

The viewpoints in *Opposing Viewpoints: Capitalism* present voices on both sides of this economic and social debate in chapters entitled "Is Capitalism in Crisis?", "What Is Capitalism's Role in Society?", "Are There Any Modern Alternatives to Capitalism?", and "Is Capitalism a Force for Moral Good?". Through considering these questions, readers will be empowered to develop an informed opinion on this persistent issue.

OPPOSING
VIEWPOINTS®
SERIES

| Is Capitalism in Crisis?

Chapter Preface

Capitalism is as omnipresent today as it has ever been, but so are its critics. If the end of the Cold War (1947–1991) between the U.S. and the communist Soviet Union seemed to bring a decisive end to a longstanding fight between two different economic systems, then the emerging problems of the new millennium seemingly restarted those conflicts and arguments all over again. For some, the free-market ideals of capitalism as a concept were getting watered down by the immense size of government infrastructure. For others, the climate crisis seemed to pose a rather direct question on the capacity of capitalism to fundamentally change how people live and make a positive change in their environmental impact.

But the system was taking new forms too. The gig economy is one such example. Did it reflect an ultimate form of economic freedom, or a process of removing any safety nets that may have existed through traditional employment? Was it a more efficient way to deliver services within the system of capitalism, or just another nefarious way to skim wages from workers?

New forms of capitalist activity brought new questions and new ways of criticizing capitalism. A growing tide of regularly occurring economic challenges made the idea of prosperity feel constantly precarious. For the critics, capitalism was in the middle of a crisis, caused in part by its previous triumphs around the world. In the place of the systems that it displaced, the infrastructure of capitalism was now tasked with fixing major systemic issues in a number of different countries, largely because there was nothing else left.

In these viewpoints, you will read about how the infrastructure of capitalism has been holding up in recent decades, from managing the world of debt to instigating action on a mass scale to combat climate change. Supporters of the system say that the capitalist center of Western society can definitely hold, and in fact, is holding pretty well. Critics argue that, on the other hand, things could easiily fall apart.

> *"Popular capitalism may have delivered a quick political win for Margaret Thatcher, but it brought no discernible impact on long run share ownership."*

Is "Popular Capitalism" Possible Today?

Paul Grout

In this viewpoint, academic Paul Grout looks to two examples in recent history of when the British government supported projects conceptualized on an idea called "popular capitalism," which involved privatizing government-owned companies and giving shares of their ownership to the employees instead. Grout is not a fan of this idea, arguing that it didn't quite work when the conversative government under then-Prime Minister Margaret Thatcher implemented it in the '80s, and that it likely wouldn't accomplish its stated goals when proposed by David Cameron, who was prime minister of the United Kingdom in the 2013, the year this viewpoint was originally published. Paul Grout is a professor at the University of Bristol, where he teaches political economy.

"'Popular Capitalism' of the 80s Returns via Royal Mail & Lloyds," by Paul Grout, The Conversation, October 16, 2013. https://theconversation.com/popular-capitalism-of-the-80s-returns-via-royal-mail-and-lloyds-19168. Licensed under CC BY ND 4.0.

As you read, consider the following questions:

1. What led economists in the 1980s to push the view that there is a logic to persuading employees to buy shares in their own companies?
2. Why does Grout say that the historical experience does not argue in favor of contemplating "another round of popular capitalism?"
3. What are some "solid economic arguments" against an economic policy that gives ordinary people incentives to become long-term holders of small, undiversified portfolios of shares, according to this viewpoint?

The past few months have seen the flotation of Royal Mail, the Lloyds share sale and the first national employee ownership day. The theme linking these three developments is one that has been around since the 1980s: the belief that everyone should own property and shares in companies.

With David Cameron directly linking the Royal Mail sale to this "popular capitalism," an idea that he says "allows everyone to share in the success of the market," it is startling to see how little has moved on over the past few decades. In particular, if the current landscape is so familiar, then surely the lessons from the past should help us navigate around today.

Back in the 80s, many economists pushed the view that there was a certain logic in persuading employees to buy shares in their own companies, rather than getting the average family to directly hold a small portfolio of shares. According to this view, the latter policy was doomed to failure in the long run.

Giving employees of newly privatised companies a large number of cheap shares had some logic. In particular, the Thatcher government saw it as a way of weakening union power and hence easing in needed changes in employment practices.

Even if employees knew the objective was to weaken their rights in the longer term, it still made sense for them to take up the deals. If no one else buys then you get a freebie on the shares and no loss of worker power. But if everyone buys, it makes no sense to give up your own bribe since the union power will be diluted anyway. Though not entirely down to the share ownership strategy, labour relations in privatised industries indeed changed dramatically after sell-offs.

More generally however, persuading workers to take up shares in their companies proved far harder. There are obvious dangers for employees because if the firm does badly not only is your job at risk but with employee ownership your wealth is going to take a hit at exactly the same time.

Someone, therefore, had to put money on the table to provide some protection against this bundling of risk, and the taxpayer duly contributed a little. But, despite the political enthusiasm, companies never responded in a big way and the model of employee ownership never really matched the hype.

Popular Capitalism

In the 80s the government's policies encouraging small-scale investors to buy up shares in privatised companies came to be known as "popular capitalism."

As a result of fears that the BT flotation in 1984 might not be a success, sweeteners were provided to the general public. People duly signed up in droves and rather liked to be given money to buy and then sell on shares. Spotting the political benefits of having a large number of share owning voters, the justification for the sweeteners in subsequent privatisations rested on popular capitalism as an end in itself, not a means of getting the job done.

There are, in any case, solid economic arguments against a policy that gives ordinary people incentives to become long-term holders of small, undiversified portfolios of shares. It leads to far greater concentration of risk and higher transactions costs than those faced by larger investors.

Hence, these small investors have to be "bribed" to hold a small portfolio without any obvious significant long run benefit to society (unlike employee share ownership which may bring some benefits to companies and the economy).

Nothing's Changed

Jump to 2013 and very little seems to have changed. The Royal Mail flotation gave about 10% of the share allocation to employees, against a backdrop of worker strikes. Whether the share allocation impacts on employee attitudes in the coming months is not certain but it would be surprising if it did not go some way towards splintering workers and hence aiding management to make changes.

Even more reminiscent of the early privatisations is the massive oversubscription of Royal Mail shares offered to private investors. Even before launch newspapers were predicting "instant profits," and published articles on the best way to move the shares on cheaply. For this flotation, the government even set in place special procedures to make this cheaper and more straightforward.

While this may make a few people happy, history suggests long term gains from this policy will be minimal or non-existent. Popular capitalism may have delivered a quick political win for Margaret Thatcher, but it brought no discernible impact on long run share ownership.

The 1990 privatisation of regional electricity companies makes the point clearly. By this point, the popular capitalism model of privatisation was well honed. There were millions of applications from private investors and the shares were so heavily oversubscribed that many missed out.

Small private investors made a quick buck and exited quickly, with 40% of the original shareholdings sold within ten months. Indeed, almost all of the electricity distribution networks are now absent from the stock market, with a current list of owners that includes Warren Buffet, JP Morgan, and Spanish utilities giant Iberdrola.

A Popular Capitalist Sale?

Next up is Lloyds Banking Group, with hints that a portion of the government's stake may be sold to retail investors.

But nothing in the Royal Mail flotation to date suggests that large, attractive, retail offerings of the government's banking stakes will end up with results any different from the 80s and 90s wider share ownership policy. Though the scale of interest in Royal Mail shares has been somewhat surprising, the main message should not be to contemplate another round of popular capitalism.

The push for increased employee ownership over the last year or so is also all very reminiscent of the enthusiasm 25 years ago. But very little came of that and it is hard to see what has changed this time round.

So what do we learn from all this déjà vu? Royal Mail is something of a one-off throwback and should be viewed in this way. The unexpected mass oversubscription from private investors and using employee share ownership in the face of union pressure all sounds familiar, but it certainly gives us no blueprint for the way to deal with the banks.

> *"The dawn of a new gig economy has seemed plausible because the Internet has been dramatically reducing transaction costs."*

The Gig Economy Has Not Killed Off Traditional Employment

Greg Rosalsky

This viewpoint by Greg Rosalsky was originally published in 2019 and takes a look at then-new numbers from the U.S. Bureau of Labor Statistics that had shown a plateauing in the growth of the number of workers who were involved in the "gig economy." By digging into the numbers, this viewpoint looks at how expectations from economists changed over the years and how the workforce has responded to an influx of brands built on using gig workers, from delivery apps to transportation apps. Looking further back, this viewpoint also considers how the "full employment" idea of labor was developed in the first place. Greg Rosalsky is a reporter for NPR's "Planet Money" podcast.

As you read, consider the following questions:

1. Why did some economists say that the gig economy had turned into "a big nothingburger" by 2019?

"Why Hasn't The Gig Economy Killed Traditional Work?" by Greg Rosalsky, NPR.org, March 26, 2019. Reprinted by permission.

2. What did supporters of the gig economy say about its decline at the time?

3. How does this viewpoint argue that the full-time employment model was seen as radical in its time?

In recent months, a slew of studies has debunked predictions that we're witnessing the dawn of a new "gig economy." The U.S. Bureau of Labor Statistics (BLS) found that there was actually a decline in the categories of jobs associated with the gig economy between 2005 and 2017. Larry Katz and the late Alan Krueger then revised their influential study that had originally found gig work was exploding. Instead, they found it had only grown modestly. Other economists ended up finding the same—and now writers are declaring the gig economy is "a big nothingburger."

The Gig Revolution's True Believer

Arun Sundararajan, a professor at the NYU Stern School of Business and the author of *The Sharing Economy: The End of Employment and the Rise of Crowd-Based Capitalism,* remains a true believer in the gig revolution. Sundararajan has been pushing the idea that the gig economy—and specifically work done through digital platforms like Uber and Airbnb—will conquer traditional employment. Instead of an economy dominated by big corporations, he believes it will be dominated by "a crowd" of self-employed entrepreneurs and workers transacting with customers through digital platforms. "We are in the early days of a fundamental reorganization of the economy," Sundararajan said while riding to the airport in, naturally, an Uber.

When asked about the onslaught of data contradicting his thesis, Sundararajan said the Bureau of Labor Statistics continues "to underestimate the size of the gig economy and in particular of the platform-based gig economy." The best BLS estimate of the number of gig workers employed through digital platforms —whether full-time, part-time or occasionally—is one percent of the total U.S. workforce, or about 1.6 million workers, as of mid-2017. Sundararajan argues that the survey questions the BLS used to gather this data were clunky and don't quite capture what's going on.

While Sundararajan disagrees with estimates about the size of the gig economy, he agrees that most people doing new gig work are either Uber and Lyft drivers or Airbnb hosts. It's no coincidence that housing and transportation have been the two main areas of growth. Homes and cars are the most valuable things many people possess, and the Internet and smartphones have made using them to make extra money much easier. Sundararajan makes a good case that there will be growth in areas like health care and accounting as well, but there is little evidence to suggest we're witnessing "the end of employment."

WHAT IS A GIG ECONOMY?

A gig economy is a work environment where organizations hire temporary workers or freelancers instead of full-time long-term employees. Companies provide temporary positions to workers and the latter reaches independent, short-term contracts with them. The trend is very strong in advanced economies like the US where there is large volume of cases where firms engages in short term contracts with workers. Even the terms employer/employees cannot be used here as it indicates a rather long-term identity.

What Promotes Gig Economy?

Now what makes firms and workers led to short-term work contracts?

A main reason is the emergence of the digital age. Here, the workforce is highly mobile and work can be done from anywhere, anytime. This means that you don't need to reach the location of the organization to do the job. The distance indeed creates a distance in relationships as well.

A second propellant factor for the gig economy is that firms, in the era of disruption, when they provide short term contracts will be safe as it avoids long term obligations like pensions and other emoluments. The worker can be relieved at any time without any friction. For the worker, short-term engagements better fit for him to search for the best opportunity.

Software and technological changes taking away human efforts also contribute to the gig economy. Declining or uncertain financial conditions and necessity to cut workers at any time also promoted companies to go for short term contracts. Temporary nature of projects and greater specializations etc., added to this trend.

Slow penetration of the millennial work culture into the labour market also encouraged short term contract engagements. Uncertain business climates and declining profits in the context of disruptive innovations also tempted companies to go for short-term labors.

In the US, colleges and universities recruit teachers and professors on a contract basis. But the typical example is the digital sector workers like the Uber workforce who have a short term and flexible contract with the organization.

The trend of the short term contract and the emergence of the gig economy have created competition and efficiency among workers, but at the same time, make the work environment uncertain for them.

In the gig economy, through short-term engagements, firms benefit from several angles. As mentioned, labour welfare emoluments like pension, gratuity etc., can be avoided. Similarly, they save training time and related expenses. The future work situation will be that of the gig economy, business analysts predicts.

"What is Gig Economy?", by Tojo Jose, Indian Economy.net, August 20, 2017.

The Resilience of Traditional Employment

Employment as a we know it is a relatively new development. At the turn of the 20th century, almost half of Americans were still self-employed as farmers and ranchers and artisans. But in the background, a mighty organization called the company was taking off. By 1960, around 85% of Americans were employees of companies.

While Sundararajan believes our economy will once again be dominated by the self-employed, he admits that full-time employment has "tons of advantages." It offers stability, a steady paycheck, and benefits. We've collectively engineered much of our social safety net around participating in this system. All of this means, Sundararajan says, "we're going to see full-time employment remain resilient, even though there are more efficient ways of organizing economic activity." He believes work done through gig platforms can be more efficient than work done in a traditional company—and that will spell the company's doom.

The Mysterious Benefits of the Firm

Economists were long confused by the existence of companies. They celebrated prices and competition—and it seemed natural that the most efficient way to do business was as individuals transacting within the open market. Need an advertiser? Hire one for a few weeks. Want design work? Work for the highest bidder until the project is done.

From this traditional view, it seemed odd that we would organize ourselves as full-time employees in top-down, bureaucratic organizations insulated from the market. Then came Ronald Coase, who won a Nobel Prize in 1991 in large part because of his 1937 paper, "The Nature of The Firm." Coase argued that the reason firms exist is that it's costly for individuals to transact in the market. You have to search for trustworthy people with quality goods or services and then haggle with them, and doing this over and over is inefficient. Within a company, Coase argued, these "transaction costs" are minimized. You can quickly walk to your colleague's desk and share ideas without having to figure out if they're shady. You can share resources, tools, and machinery. You can work in a team and specialize in different tasks. And you can do this all without having to continually negotiate over the price of everything.

The dawn of a new gig economy has seemed plausible because the Internet has been dramatically reducing transaction costs. Search engines have made it incredibly cheap to find goods and services, compare prices, and get bargains. Social media and peer reviews have made it easier to determine if people are trustworthy.

E-commerce has made it easier to process payments. You can click a button on a mobile phone and instantaneously have GPS guide drivers right to you. But as big as these efficiency gains have been, a new economy based on crowds of people doing gigs through digital platforms—as exciting or scary as that might sound—still doesn't compare to one based on the efficiencies and stability of the good old-fashioned company.

> *"The public debate takes on its usual binary, black-and-white, conflict-oriented, unproductive and basically incorrect form. Such a debate feeds into a growing distrust many have for capitalism."*

How Capitalism Fights Climate Change

Andrew J. Hoffman

In this viewpoint, Andrew J. Hoffman makes the case that the capitalist system is equipped with the economic tools needed to address issues like climate change. In fact, he argues that efforts to suggest that the system needs to change in some way are largely a distraction from focusing on how the system actually does work and all the things that it is already accomplishing, like adjusting to a changing climate. There is simply no other way to deal with the challenges presented by climate change, according to this viewpoint. Andrew J. Hoffman is a professor who teaches sustainable enterprise at the University of Michigan.

As you read, consider the following questions:

1. What do you think the author means by the "culture wars?"

2. Why does this author think that "this binary framing" hides some of the real underlying issues involving climate change?

3. In what ways does this viewpoint argue that capitalism is "quite malleable" to meet the needs of society?

There are two extremes in the debate over capitalism's role in our present climate change problem. On the one hand, some people see climate change as the outcome of a consumerist market system run rampant. In the end, the result will be a call to replace capitalism with a new system that will correct our present ills with regulations to curb market excesses.

On the other hand, some people have faith in a free market to yield the needed solutions to our social problems. In the more extreme case, some see climate policy as a covert way for bigger government to interfere in the market and diminish citizens' personal freedom.

Between these two extremes, the public debate takes on its usual binary, black-and-white, conflict-oriented, unproductive and basically incorrect form. Such a debate feeds into a growing distrust many have for capitalism.

A 2013 survey found that only 54% of Americans had a positive view of the term, and in many ways both the Occupy and Tea Party movements share similar distrust in the macro-institutions of our society to serve everyone fairly; one focuses its ire at government, the other at big business, and both distrust what they see as a cozy relationship between the two.

This polar framing also feeds into culture wars that are taking place in our country. Studies have shown that conservative-leaning people are more likely to be skeptical of climate change, due in part to a belief that this would necessitate controls on industry and commerce, a future they do not want. Indeed, research has shown a strong correlation between support for free-market ideology and rejection of climate science. Conversely, liberal-leaning people are more likely to believe in climate change because, in part, solutions are consistent with resentment toward commerce and industry and the damage they cause to society.

This binary framing masks the real questions we face, both what we need to do and how we are going to get there. Yet there are serious conversations within management education, research and practice about the next steps in the evolution of capitalism. The goal is to develop a more sophisticated notion of the role of the corporation within society. These discussions are being driven not only by climate change, but concerns raised by the financial crisis, growing income inequality and other serious social issues.

The Market's Rough Edges

Capitalism is a set of institutions for structuring our commerce and interaction. It is not, as some think, some sort of natural state that exists free from government intrusion. It is designed by human beings in the service of human beings and it can evolve to the needs of human beings. As Yuval Levin points out in National Affairs, even Adam Smith argued that "the rules of the market are not self-legislating or naturally obvious. On the contrary, Smith argued, the market is a public institution that requires rules imposed upon it by legislators who understand its workings and its benefits."

And, it is worth noting, capitalism has been quite successful. Over the past century, the world's population increased by a factor of four, the world economy increased by a factor of 14 and global per capita income tripled. In that time, average life expectancy increased by almost two-thirds due in large part to advances in medicine, shelter, food production and other amenities provided by the market economy.

Capitalism is, in fact, quite malleable to meet the needs of society as they emerge. Over time, regulation has evolved to address emergent issues such as monopoly power, collusion, price-fixing and a host of other impediments to the needs of society. Today, one of those needs is responding to climate change.

The question is not whether capitalism works or doesn't work. The question is how it can and will evolve to address the new challenges we face as a society. Or, as Anand Giridharadas pointed out at the Aspen Action Forum, "Capitalism's rough edges must be sanded and its surplus fruit shared, but the underlying system must never be questioned."

These rough edges need be considered with the theories we use to understand and teach the market. In addition, we need to reconsider the metrics we use to measure its outcomes, and the ways in which the market has deviated from its intended form.

Homo economicus?

To begin, there are growing questions around the underlying theories and models used to understand, explain and set policies for the market. Two that have received significant attention are neoclassical economics and principal-agent theory. Both theories form the foundation of management education and practice and are built on extreme and rather dismal simplifications of human beings as largely untrustworthy and driven by avarice, greed and selfishness.

As regards neoclassical economics, Eric Beinhocker and Nick Hanauer explain:

> "Behavioral economists have accumulated a mountain of evidence showing that real humans don't behave as a rational homo economicus would. Experimental economists have raised awkward questions about the very existence of utility; and that is problematic because it has long been the device economists use to show that markets maximize social welfare. Empirical economists have identified anomalies suggesting that financial markets aren't always efficient."

As regards principal-agent theory, Lynn Stout goes so far to say that the model is quite simply "wrong." The Cornell professor of business and law argues that its central premise—that those running the company (agents) will shirk or even steal from the owner (principal) since they do the work and the owner gets the profits—does not capture "the reality of modern public corporations with thousands of shareholders, scores of executives and a dozen or more directors."

The most pernicious outcome of these models is the idea that the purpose of the corporation is to "make money for its shareholders." This is a rather recent idea that began to take hold within business only in the 1970s and 1980s and has now become a taken-for-granted assumption.

If I asked any business school student (and perhaps any American) to complete the sentence, "the purpose of the corporation is to…" they would parrot "make money for the shareholder." But that is not what a company does, and most executives would tell you so. Companies transform ideas and innovation into products and services that serve the needs of some segment of the market. In the words of Paul Pollman, CEO of Unilever, "business is here to serve society." Profit is the metric for how well they do that.

The problem with the pernicious notion that a corporation's sole purpose is to serve shareholders is that it leads to many other undesirable outcomes. For example, it leads to an increased focus on quarterly earnings and short-term share price swings; it limits the latitude of strategic thinking by decreasing focus on long-term investment and strategic planning; and it rewards only the type of shareholder who, in the words of Lynn Stout, is "shortsighted, opportunistic, willing to impose external costs, and indifferent to ethics and others' welfare."

A Better Way to Gauge the Economy

Going beyond our understanding of what motivates people and organizations within the market, there is growing attention to the metrics that guide the outcomes of that action. One of those metrics is the discount rate. Economist Nicholas Stern stirred a healthy controversy when he used an unusually low discount rate when calculating the future costs and benefits of climate change mitigation and adaptation, arguing that there is a ethical component to this metric's use. For example, a common discount rate of 5% leads to a conclusion that everything 20 years out and beyond is worthless. When gauging the response to climate change, is that an outcome that anyone—particularly anyone with children or grandchildren—would consider ethical?

Another metric is gross domestic product (GDP), the foremost economic indicator of national economic progress. It is a measure of all financial transactions for products and services. But one problem is that it does not acknowledge (nor value) a distinction between those transactions that add to the well-being of a country and those that diminish it. Any activity in which money changes hands will register as GDP growth. GDP treats the recovery from natural disasters as economic gain; GDP increases with polluting activities and then again with pollution cleanup; and it treats all depletion of natural capital as income, even when the depreciation of that capital asset can limit future growth.

A second problem with GDP is that it is not a metric dealing with true human well-being at all. Instead, it is based on the tacit assumption that the more money and wealth we have, the better off we are. But that's been challenged by numerous studies.

As a result, French ex-president Nicolas Sarkozy created a commission, headed by Joseph Stieglitz and Amartya Sen (both Nobel laureates), to examine alternatives to GDP. Their report recommended a shift in economic emphasis from simply the production of goods to a broader measure of overall well-being that would include measures for categories like health, education and security. It also called for greater focus on the societal effects of income inequality, new ways to measure the economic impact of sustainability and ways to include the value of wealth to be passed on to the next generation. Similarly, the king of Bhutan has developed a GDP alternative called gross national happiness, which is a composite of indicators that are much more directly related to human well-being than monetary measures.

The form of capitalism we have today has evolved over centuries to reflect growing needs, but also has been warped by private interests. Yuval Levin points out that some key moral features of

Adam Smith's political economy have been corrupted in more recent times, most notably by "a growing collusion between government and large corporations." This issue has become most vivid after the financial crisis and the failed policies that both preceded and succeeded that watershed event. The answers, as Auden Schendler and Mark Trexler point out, are both "policy solutions" and "corporations to advocate for those solutions."

We Can Never Have a Clean Slate

How will we get to the solutions for climate change? Let's face it. Installing efficient LED light bulbs, driving the latest Tesla electric car and recycling our waste are admirable and desirable activities. But they are not going to solve the climate problem by reducing our collective emissions to a necessary level. To achieve that goal requires systemic change. To that end, some argue for creating a new system to replace capitalism. For example, Naomi Klein calls for "shredding the free-market ideology that has dominated the global economy for more than three decades."

Klein is performing a valuable service with her call for extreme action. She, like Bill McKibben and his 350.org movement, is helping to make it possible for a conversation to take place over the magnitude of the challenge before us through what is called the "radical flank effect."

All members and ideas of a social movement are viewed in contrast to others, and extreme positions can make other ideas and organizations seem more reasonable to movement opponents. For example, when Martin Luther King Jr first began speaking his message, it was perceived as too radical for the majority of white America. But when Malcolm X entered the debate, he pulled the radical flank further out and made King's message look more moderate by comparison. Capturing this sentiment, Russell Train, second administrator of the EPA, once quipped, "Thank God for [environmentalist] Dave Brower; he makes it so easy for the rest of us to be reasonable."

But the nature of social change never allows us the clean slate that makes sweeping statements for radical change attractive. Every set of institutions by which society is structured evolved from some set of structures that preceded it. Stephen Jay Gould made this point quite powerfully in his essay "The Creation Myths of Cooperstown," where he pointed out that baseball was not invented by Abner Doubleday in Cooperstown New York in 1839. In fact, he points out, "no one invented baseball at any moment or in any spot." It evolved from games that came before it. In a similar way, Adam Smith did not invent capitalism in 1776 with his book *The Wealth of Nations*. He was writing about changes that he was observing and had been taking place for centuries in European economies; most notably the division of labor and the improvements in efficiency and quality of production that were the result.

In the same way, we cannot simply invent a new system to replace capitalism. Whatever form of commerce and interchange we adopt must evolve out of the form we have at the present. There is simply no other way.

But one particularly difficult challenge of climate change is that, unlike Adam Smith's proverbial butcher, brewer or baker who provide our dinner out of the clear alignment of their self-interest and our needs, climate change breaks the link between action and outcome in profound ways. A person or corporation cannot learn about climate change through direct experience. We cannot feel an increase in global mean temperature; we cannot see, smell or taste greenhouse gases; and we cannot link an individual weather anomaly with global climate shifts.

A real appreciation of the issue requires an understanding of large-scale systems through "big data" models. Moreover, both the knowledge of these models and an appreciation for how they work require deep scientific knowledge about complex dynamic systems and the ways in which feedback loops in the climate system, time delays, accumulations and nonlinearities operate within them. Therefore, the evolution of capitalism to address climate change must, in many ways, be based on trust, belief and faith in stakeholders outside the normal exchange of commerce. To get to the next iteration of this centuries-old institution, we must envision the market through all components that help to establish the rules; corporations, government, civil society, scientists and others.

The Evolving Role of the Corporation in Society

At the end of the day, the solutions to climate change must come from the market and more specifically, from business. The market is the most powerful institution on earth, and business is the most powerful entity within it. Business makes the goods and services we rely upon: the clothes we wear, the food we eat, the forms of mobility we use and the buildings we live and work in.

Businesses can transcend national boundaries and possess resources that exceed that of many countries. You can lament that fact, but it is a fact. If business does not lead the way toward solutions for a carbon-neutral world, there will be no solutions.

Capitalism can, indeed it must, evolve to address our current climate crisis. This cannot happen through either wiping clean the institutions that presently exist or relying on the benevolence of a laissez faire market. It will require thoughtful leaders creating a thoughtfully structured market.

> *"But 'climate crisis' signifies something that feels beyond the range of ordinary experience, especially to the wealthy. People quickly reach for culturally available ideas to fill the vacuum."*

Capitalism's Constant "Crisis"

Noel Castree

This viewpoint by Noel Castree takes a look at the language that capitalist societies use to describe the ongoing climate "crisis." Language that was once primarily used by activists on the fringes of political activity has now been commandeered by people with the reins of political power too. This viewpoint meditates on whether that suggests the system can meet the needs of the moment, or if it just reflects exaggeration and sensationalism. The reality of what the climate "crisis" will look like is less likely to be reminiscent of a scene pulled from apocalyptic fiction or rhetoric, but it will still be a significant problem. Noel Castree is a professor at the University of Technology Sydney, where he teaches classes on society and the environment.

"The Climate Crisis Is Real – but Overusing Terms Like 'Crisis' and 'Emergency' Comes with Risk," by Noel Castree, The Conversation, September 11, 2022. https://theconversation.com/the-climate-crisis-is-real-but-overusing-terms-like-crisis-and-emergency-comes-with-risk-188750. Licensed under CC BY 4.0 International.

As you read, consider the following questions:

1. According to Castree, what kinds of terms are getting used a lot to describe the impacts of global warming?
2. Does this writer think that apocalyptic narratives are helpful or harmful in the larger debate over climate change?
3. How does this viewpoint define the word "crisis?"

"

C risis" is an incredibly potent word, so it's interesting to witness the way the phrase "climate crisis" has become part of the lingua franca.

Once associated only with a few "outspoken" scientists and activists, the phrase has now gone mainstream.

But what do people understand by the term "climate crisis"? And why does it matter?

The Mainstreaming of Crisis-Talk

It's not only activists or scientists sounding the alarm.

UN Secretary General Antonio Guterres now routinely employs dramatic phrases like "digging our own graves" when discussing climate. Bill Gates advises us to avoid "climate disaster."

This linguistic mainstreaming marks redrawn battle lines in the "climate wars."

Denialism is in retreat. The climate change debate now is about what is to be done and by whom?

Scientists, using the full authority of their profession, have been key to changing the discourse. The lead authors of the Intergovernmental Panel on Climate Change (IPCC) reports now pull no punches, talking openly about mass starvation, extinctions and disasters.

These public figures clearly hope to jolt citizens, businesses and governments into radical climate action.

But for many ordinary folks, climate change can seem remote from everyday life. It's not a "crisis" in the immediate way the pandemic has been.

Of course, many believe climate experts have understated the problem for too long.

And yet the new ubiquity of siren terms like climate "crisis", "emergency", "disaster", "breakdown" and "calamity" does not guarantee any shared, let alone credible, understanding of their possible meaning.

This matters because such terms tend to polarise.

Few now doubt the reality of climate change. But how we describe its implications can easily repeat earlier stand-offs between "believers" and "sceptics"; "realists' and "scare-mongerers." The result is yet more political inertia and gridlock.

We will need to do better.

Four Ideas for a New Way Forward

Terms like "climate crisis" are here to stay. But scientists, teachers and politicians need to be savvy. A keen awareness of what other people may think when they hear us shout "crisis!" can lead to better communication.

Here are four ideas to keep in mind.

1. We Must Challenge Dystopian and Salvation Narratives

A crisis is when things fall apart. We see news reports of crises daily— floods in Pakistan, economic collapse in Sri Lanka, famine in parts of Africa.

But "climate crisis" signifies something that feels beyond the range of ordinary experience, especially to the wealthy. People quickly reach for culturally available ideas to fill the vacuum.

One is the notion of an all-encompassing societal break down, where only a few survive. Cormac McCarthy's bleak book *The Road* is one example.

Central to many apocalyptic narratives is the idea technology and a few brave people (usually men) can save the day in the nick of time, as in films like *Interstellar*.

The problem, of course, is these (often fanciful) depictions aren't suitable ways to interpret what climate scientists have been warning people about. The world is far more complicated.

2. We Must Bring the Climate Crisis
Home and Make It Present *Now*

Even if they're willing to acknowledge it as a looming crisis, many think climate change impacts will be predominantly felt elsewhere or in the distant future.

The disappearance of Tuvalu as sea levels rise is an existential crisis for its citizens but may seem a remote, albeit tragic, problem to people in Chicago, Oslo or Cape Town.

But the recent floods in eastern Australia and the heatwave in Europe allow a powerful point to be made: no place is immune from extreme weather as the planet heats up.

There won't be a one-size-fits-all global climate crisis as per many Hollywood movies. Instead, people must understand global warming will trigger myriad local-to-regional scale crises.

Many will be on the doorstep, many will last for years or decades. Most will be made worse if we don't act now. Getting people to understand this is crucial.

3. We Must Explain: A Crisis in Relation to What?

The climate wars showed us value disputes get transposed into arguments about scientific evidence and its interpretation.

A crisis occurs when events are judged in light of certain values, such as people's right to adequate food, healthcare and shelter.

Pronouncements of crisis need to explain the values that underpin judgements about unacceptable risk, harm and loss.

Historians, philosophers, legal scholars and others help us to think clearly about our values and what exactly we mean when we say "crisis."

4. We Must Appreciate Other Crises and Challenges Matter More to Many People

Some are tempted to occupy the moral high ground and imply the climate crisis is so grand as to eclipse all others. This is understandable but imprudent.

It's important to respect other perspectives and negotiate a way forward. Consider, for example, the way author Bjørn Lomborg has questioned the climate emergency by arguing it's not the main threat.

Lomborg was widely pilloried. But his arguments resonated with many. We may disagree with him, but his views are not irrational.

We must seek to understand how and why this kind of argument makes sense to so many people.

Words matter. It's vital terms like "crisis" and "calamity" don't become rhetorical devices devoid of real content as we argue about what climate action to take.

> "Ocean acidification, freshwater use,
> and land use are likewise teetering at
> the precipice of disaster. And yet, in
> the face of this potential catastrophe,
> capitalism would have us only
> grow more."

Capitalism's Focus on Growth Makes It Incompatible with Fighting Climate Change

Alyssa Rohricht

In this viewpoint, Alyssa Rohricht argues that the central goal of capitalism is to build profits. In theory, this means that if individuals build profits, the market will grow, and society will reap the benefits. In reality, though, Rohricht says that capitalism is not equipped to deal with societal ills ranging from poverty to human rights. One of the problems facing society that capitalism seems to be worsening is climate change. Under capitalism, production needs to constantly increase for the economy to be considered healthy, but unfortunately this means higher carbon emissions and other harmful environmental practices. Alyssa Rohricht is a writer who maintains the Black Cat Revolution blog.

"Capitalism and Climate Change," by Alyssa Rohricht, CounterPunch, May 29, 2014. Reprinted by permission.

As you read, consider the following questions:

1. Why does the ecological economist Herman Daly call the concept of sustainable growth a "bad oxymoron?"
2. According to data cited from the Worldwatch Institute, how many people could Earth support if everyone consumed at the rate of the average American?
3. What is John Stuart Mill's "stationary state," and how does Rohricht believe it would function in a capitalist economy?

Capitalism dominates the globe. It has become so enmeshed into the cultural narrative that it seems almost axiomatic. Private owners (of capital) control the means of production. The goal: build profits. The best part about it is that if everyone pursues self-interest, the market will grow and society will benefit. The invisible hand helps the market to self-regulate, creating socially desirable results.

Simple?

No. When it comes to dealing with issues such as poverty, the income gap, unemployment, economic crises, human rights, war, imperialism, and the externalization of costs on society and the environment, the invisible hand that Adam Smith once imagined is not invisible, it is nonexistent.

We are currently experiencing, without a doubt, the greatest crisis to face human kind. Indications of climate change are being seen around the globe: accelerated melting of the Arctic sea ice, rapidly receding glaciers, rising sea levels, warming oceans and ocean acidification, more frequent and longer-lasting droughts, stronger and more frequent storms, higher temperatures than ever recorded, and a rapid extinction of species are direct result of a warming climate.

There is a scientific consensus that the climate is rapidly changing and that these rapid changes are due to anthropogenic causes. The science is clear: the human-caused emissions of great amounts of greenhouse gases—primarily carbon dioxide, methane, and nitrous oxide—are causing global environmental damage.

Many argue that market and tech-based approaches are the way to combat climate change. They push for carbon taxing and trading, geo-engineering, and renewable energy without considering the fact that the system itself is incompatible with sustainability. By its very nature, capitalism seeks only to grow and accumulate—an idea that is diametrically opposed to a sustainable existence.

In this series, I will examine how the capitalist system has brought us to climate disaster, and why it cannot get us out of it.

The Growth Problem

Ecological economist Herman Daly perhaps best emphasized the issue of unlimited economic growth acting within a limited environment. He called the idea of sustainable growth a "bad oxymoron" that is simply impossible.

"Impossibility statements are the very foundation of science. It is impossible to: travel faster than the speed of light; create or destroy matter-energy; build a perpetual motion machine, etc. By respecting impossibility theorems we avoid wasting resources on projects that are bound to fail. Therefore economists should be very interested in impossibility theorems, especially the one to be demonstrated here, namely that it is impossible for the world economy to grow its way out of poverty and environmental degradation. In other words, sustainable growth is impossible."

Earth's ecosystem is finite, yet our culture has developed a system whereby economic stability is gained only through unlimited growth. Within the capitalist market system, growth is essential, and the larger the growth, the healthier the economy. When growth slows, or worse, stops entirely, the system is in crisis.

Ecological health, on the other hand, is experiencing its own crisis as climate change threatens the stability of the entire planet. We've already exceeded the earth's carrying capacity, and yet unfettered growth of the world's population and greater resource consumption have continued. The Worldwatch Institute estimated that if the world consumed resources at the same rate per person as the average person in the United States, the Earth could support only 1.4 billion people. A world population of 6.2 billion (a number we've already far exceeded) could only support an average per capita income at about $5,100 per year. In the US, the average income per year is about $28,000.

Yet reducing our consumptive habits is antithetical to the capitalist enterprise, which functions only if the economy is growing. We have created a world system where economic health is directly opposed to environmental health. Capitalism necessitates ever increasing resource use, while the natural capacities of the environment require a severe cutback in consumption.

John Stuart Mill recognized this problem early on. He saw that capitalism's focus on unlimited growth within a limited environment would logically lead to immense environmental destruction. Yet, instead of dismissing the system all together, Mill argued for a "stationary state", or a state where economic growth ceases.

"If the earth must lose that great portion of its pleasantness which it owes to things that the unlimited increase of wealth and population would extirpate from it, for the mere purpose of enabling it to support a larger but not a better or a happier population, I sincerely hope, for the sake of posterity, that they will be content to be stationary, long before necessity compels them to it."

Yet a stationary state would mean certain disaster for a capitalist economy. Growth is simply essential for its survival. Spurred on by competition, capitalism seeks to constantly re-invest surplus into more capital; a system of self-expansion seeking only greater accumulation. The concept of stationary capitalism is an oxymoron.

Not only does capitalism need to expand its resource production and consumption, it also must seek out new markets in which to establish itself. Population growth is basic to capitalism, which is always seeking to grow the labor force and increase production of goods and thus capital. Growth in population means demands increase for new housing, furniture, appliances, schools, roads, cars, agriculture, and so forth, creating a healthier capitalist economy at the great expense of the environment and all species that inhabit it. The more people there are to purchase a car and fill it with gasoline, the more money that floods the market. The more people we can get hooked on iPads, yearly cellphone upgrades, shoes, and makeup.

Directly opposed to the constant need for growth are Earth's natural systems and carrying capacity. Scientists at the Stockholm Resilience Centre analyzed several of earth's systems and calculated the "planetary boundaries" for each that are vital to maintaining an environment livable for humans. Many of these boundaries have already been exceeded. In the case of carbon dioxide, the preindustrial value was 280 parts per million (ppm) concentrated in the atmosphere. The planetary boundary is estimated at 350 ppm. Currently, the earth is at 390 ppm.

The measurements for biodiversity loss read similarly dire. Some of the systems measured for the planetary boundary have not yet been surpassed, yet the data is hardly comforting: the phosphorus cycle (the quantity flowing into the oceans) had a preindustrial value of 1 million tons; the boundary is estimated at 11 million tons; and the current status is 8.5 to 9.5 million tons.

Ocean acidification, freshwater use, and land use are likewise teetering at the precipice of disaster. And yet, in the face of this potential catastrophe, capitalism would have us only grow more. Land use for agriculture and development are encouraged in order to grow the economy and increase capital, freshwater is being used at alarming rates for industrial production and industrial farming, rivers, lakes, and the oceans are being polluted with plastics, heavy metals, runoff from farmlands using pesticides and other chemicals, and as temperatures increase from the burning of fossil fuels, the temperature of the planet rises, further increasing ocean acidification and permafrost melt. This "healthy" economy is leading to a very unhealthy planet.

> *"It's understandable why young folks may view revolutions as more exciting than reforms. But we need our future leaders to be open to the reality that meaningful and lasting change will be incremental. Patience and commitment are required."*

Reformers Can Improve the Economic Future in Ways Revolutionaries Cannot

David Weitzner

In this viewpoint, David Weitzner acknowledges that capitalism as it currently exists is not working, but that capitalism does not have to be entirely thrown out. Instead, it simply needs to be revitalized. He argues that younger adults—primarily Gen Z and millennials—have the power to reform capitalism. Currently, studies indicate that they do not trust corporations and institutions in general. While it is tempting and understandable for young people to want drastic, revolutionary changes to occur, slower reform is more likely to have a positive impact on the system by forcing a shift in focus from profits to high-quality products and jobs. David Weitzner is an assistant professor of administrative studies at York University, Canada.

As you read, consider the following questions:

1. According to research from Ethisphere cited in the viewpoint, what percent of Gen Z respondents chose not to report misconduct from colleagues at work?
2. According to Weitzner, why would these respondents choose not to report misconduct?
3. What did a 2022 survey cited in this viewpoint find about the American and Canadian public's trust for business leaders?

Many of our capitalist institutions have been damaged by cronyism, greed and a short-term mindset. But capitalism is more than its faults and the unpleasant outcomes brought on by a selfish class.

Revitalizing capitalism begins with reform, which means introducing changes within the existing structure. However, the newest cohort to enter corporate life, Gen Z, has little confidence in the corporate system. They are unwilling to play a game where they don't trust the rules or referees.

While we don't have an extensive amount of research on this cohort, we do know that Gen Z seems to be less involved in civil engagement and reluctant to engage in teamwork.

And according to a recent study from Ethisphere, Gen Z both embraces the strongest ethical commitments and is the least likely to report bad behaviour at work. Nearly 39 per cent of Gen Z respondents chose not to report misconduct when they witnessed it—an 11-point gap from their Gen X and Boomer colleagues.

Gen Z employees don't believe reporting corporate misbehaviour is worthwhile because they fear retaliation and have no confidence corrective action will be taken. So how can Gen Z be effective agents of reform in a system they don't believe in?

Why Trust Matters

The Ethisphere study found that the younger the employee, the less confidence they had in corporate anti-retaliation policies. This finding is echoed by broader data showing that Gen Z doesn't trust institutions in general. Why does this matter?

Scholarly research explains that corporations are driven by institutional logics—socially constructed, historical patterns of practices, values and rules that guide day-to-day action in a corporate environment.

These institutional logics correspond to historical imprints of past environments. Imprinting goes beyond history itself—the effects of imprints vary over time, reflecting an interplay of the past and the present, as they persist despite changes in the social environment.

Organizations adhere to these imprinted logics to enhance their image and help us better understand our social environment and the parameters for how we should act.

Resistance to, and criticism of, outdated institutional logics has led to an environment amenable to change. For example, there was a time when the dominant institutional logic about the purpose of a firm was only to increase profits.

But over decades of resistance and criticism, we have arrived at a new logic where the purpose of the corporation has been redefined to include all stakeholders—not just shareholders.

The shift from shareholder to stakeholder logics represents a complete reversal of earlier institutional mindsets. The old ways of doing things, ingrained as they may be, are now challenged when corporate leaders get confronted with new ways of doing and seeing things.

No Shortcut to Transformation

While taken-for-granted beliefs and habitual practices are finally being questioned, the change is slow. Institutional theory research tells us that conflict between old and new values will be resolved through episodic change.

This kind of change involves periods of openness when one can affect meaningful change, interspersed with periods of stability when change doesn't occur.

It's understandable why young folks may view revolutions as more exciting than reforms. But we need our future leaders to be open to the reality that meaningful and lasting change will be incremental. Patience and commitment are required.

Change will come from millennials expecting capitalist enterprises to prioritize high-quality products and jobs over profit and all workers demanding better working conditions from their organizations.

And it will happen when those who see through the recent explosion of standards and products that have added complexity to business ethics—without improving ethical performance—refuse to buy in.

Win Back the Young with Trust

Gen Z is right not to trust the system as it stands. Writer and political commentator David Frum explained to me a few years back that "any reform coalition needs to take very seriously the problems of the young."

Frum observed that, so long as the elite illustrates that "'capitalism' means stagnant living standards, college debt, unaffordable childcare, impending environmental catastrophe," they will seek alternatives.

And it's not just Gen Z who has lost trust. A 2022 survey from the United States found that public trust in business leaders and politicians has also reached historic lows. A Canadian survey from a year earlier highlighted a similar trend.

Perhaps more worrisome is a poll finding that only a third of Canadians believe their fellow citizens can be trusted, no matter what their identity.

Trust has been defined as "the mutual confidence that no party to an exchange will exploit another's vulnerabilities." In contrast, "trustworthiness" can be understood as "the attribute of being worthy of the trust of others in not exploiting any adverse selection, moral hazard, holdup or other exchange vulnerability."

Under conventional capitalist thinking, it's worth being trustworthy if it leads to cost savings. We need to depart from this reductionist view.

When the youth don't trust the system, the highest priority of the establishment must be rebuilding that trust. Seeking to be seen as trustworthy is what will convince the next generation skeptical of our institutions to work with us on reform.

> *"Since its conception, the idea of late capitalism has chiefly referred to the latest stage of capitalist development. This 'last stage' condition has been bestowed on almost every period following a moment of economic crisis."*

Late Capitalism Doesn't Necessarily Mean Capitalism Is Near Its End

David Aviles Espinoza

In this viewpoint, David Aviles Espinoza explains the concept of late capitalism. Though the concept of late capitalism is said to originate with Karl Marx, it was actually Werner Sombart who coined the term in the early 20th century. Sombart asserted that late capitalism comes about after major crises, such as World War I. Since then, other theorists have expanded the term to also include the growth of multinational companies after wars and the accumulation of wealth in the hands of the privileged few. It is also characterized by increased investment in non-traditional areas, such as credit and immaterial resources. However, despite the fact that some people are trying to envision a stage after late capitalism, the past century indicates that late capitalism might be hard to leave behind. At the time this viewpoint was published, David Aviles Espinoza was a PhD candidate in political economy at the University of Sydney, Australia.

"We Live in a Time of 'Late Capitalism.' But What Does That Mean? And What's So Late About It?" by David Aviles Espinoza, The Conversation, December 7, 2022. https://theconversation.com/we-live-in-a-time-of-late-capitalism-but-what-does-that-mean-and-whats-so-late-about-it-191422. Licensed under CC BY-ND 4.0 International.

As you read, consider the following questions:

1. According to Werner Sombart, what is late capitalism?
2. According to Ernest Mandel, does late capitalism represent an essential change in the nature of capitalism?
3. What example does the author give of Frederic Jameson's claim that late capitalism includes the commodification of immaterial dimensions?

The term "late capitalism" seems to be everywhere as a trending meme—often used as a kind of shorthand to illustrate the absurdities of certain free market economies.

On Twitter, you will find the hashtags #latecapitalism (English), #tardocapitalismo (Italian), #capitalismotardio (Spanish), and #spätkapitalismus (German), among others. Typically, they satirise notions such as the idea of endless growth.

The term also pops up in a wide range of academic articles and books. There are, for instance, discussions around the populist rise in late capitalism, the increase in financial-related investments in late capitalism, migration conditions in late capitalism, and so on.

But what are the origins of this term? And what, exactly, does it mean?

The Origins

Karl Marx first analysed the last stage of capitalism in his three-volume magnum opus *Capital: A Critique of Political Economy* (published in 1867, 1885, and 1894), particularly in Volume 3.

For Marx, an acceleration in the turnover of capital, concentrating wealth in the hands of the few, would result in a continuous tendency to crises. This, he believed, would ultimately make the system collapse.

However, Marx did not use the term "late capitalism." It was coined by Werner Sombart, a controversial German historical economist, almost a century ago in his three-volume magnum opus *Der Moderne Kapitalismus* (published from 1902 through 1927).

Sombart's main contribution was to define three periods of the capitalist economic system: early or proto capitalism, advanced capitalism and late capitalism. In Sombart's analysis, late capitalism referred specifically to economic, political and social deprivations associated with the aftermath of the first world war.

A New Epoch

The term wasn't taken up widely until Belgian Marxist economist Ernest Mandel's treatise *Late Capitalism* was published in English in 1975.

Mandel used the idea to describe the economic expansion after the second world war. This was a time characterised by the emergence of multinational companies, a growth in the global circulation of capital and an increase in corporate profits and the wealth of certain individuals, chiefly in the West.

As Mandel described it, the period of late capitalism did not represent a change in the essence of capitalism, only a new epoch marked by expansion and acceleration in production and exchange. Thus one of the main features of late capitalism is the increasing amounts of capital investments into non-traditional productive areas, such as the expansion of credit.

This period of exceptional economic growth, argued Mandel, would reach its limit by the mid 1970s. At this time, the world economy was experiencing an oil crisis (in 1973, and a second wave in 1979). Britain was also experiencing a banking crisis derived from a fall in property prices and an increase in interest rates.

However, since the time of Mandel's writing such crises have become recurrent.

For instance, the 1980s were known for the different regional financial crises, such as in Latin America, the US and Japan. In 1997, we saw the Asian financial crisis. The 2008 US subprime crisis became the Great Recession.

The Cultural Component

The term "late capitalism" regained relevance in 1991 when Marxist literary critic Fredric Jameson published *Postmodernism or the Cultural Logic of Late Capitalism.*

Drawing on Mandel's idea that capitalism has sped up and gone global, Jameson expanded his analysis to the cultural realm. His argument was that late capitalist societies have lost their connection with history and are defined by a fascination with the present.

In Jameson's account, late capitalism is characterised by a globalised, post-industrial economy, where everything—not just material resources and products but also immaterial dimensions, such as the arts and lifestyle activities—becomes commodified and consumable.

In this capitalist stage, we see innovation for the sake of innovation, a superficial projected image of self via celebrities or "influencers" channelled through social media, and so on.

In this time, whatever societal changes that emerge are quickly transformed into products for exchange. Unlike those who celebrate postmodernism as replete with irony and transgression, Jameson considers it to be a non-threatening feature of the capitalist system in contemporary societies.

More recently, Jonathan Crary, in his book *Late Capitalism and the Ends of Sleep*, argues our current version of 24/7 capitalism, enabled by intrusive technologies and social media, is eroding basic human needs such as sufficient sleep. It is also eliminating "the useless time of reflection and contemplation."

And Then What?

Since its conception, the idea of late capitalism has chiefly referred to the latest stage of capitalist development. This "last stage" condition has been bestowed on almost every period following a moment of economic crisis.

Global economic upheavals such as the 2008 subprime crisis and the financial upheaval caused by the COVID-19 pandemic have led to a simultaneous expansion and concentration of wealth.

In other words, the rich get richer, and the poor get poorer, such is the ever-turning gyre of capitalism. Indeed, contemporary economists, such as Thomas Piketty and Joseph Stiglitz suggest increasing inequality could endanger our future.

What will come after late capitalism? In the face of the climate crisis, some are imagining everyday lives no longer guided by overconsumption and environmental degradation: a post-capitalist society. In the meantime, the hashtags continue.

Periodical and Internet Sources Bibliography

The following articles have been selected to supplement the diverse views presented in this chapter.

Clive Crook, "A Crisis of Leadership, Not a Crisis of Capitalism: Clive Crook," *Bloomberg,* January 3, 2012. https://www.bloomberg.com/opinion/articles/2012-01-04/crisis-of-leadership-not-crisis-of-capitalism-commentary-by-clive-crook.

Matthew Desmond, "In Order to Understand the Brutality of American Capitalism, You Have to Start on the Plantation," the *New York Times*, August 14, 2019. https://www.nytimes.com/interactive/2019/08/14/magazine/slavery-capitalism.html.

Benjamin Y. Fong, "The Climate Crisis? It's Capitalism, Stupid," the *New York Times*, November 20, 2017. https://www.nytimes.com/2017/11/20/opinion/climate-capitalism-crisis.html.

Neil Irwin, "The Pandemic Is Showing Us How Capitalism Is Amazing, and Inadequate," the *New York Times,* November 14, 2020. https://www.nytimes.com/2020/11/14/upshot/coronavirus-capitalism-vaccine.html.

Nicholas Lemann, "Is Capitalism Racist?," *New Yorker*, May 25, 2020. https://www.newyorker.com/magazine/2020/05/25/is-capitalism-racist.

James Mackintosh, "In Stakeholder Capitalism, Shareholders Are Still King," *Wall Street Journal*, Janurary 19, 2020: https://www.wsj.com/articles/in-stakeholder-capitalism-shareholders-are-still-king-11579462427.

James Mackintosh, "Will Covid-19 Shake Up Capitalism?," *Wall Street Journal*, January 17, 2021. https://www.wsj.com/articles/will-covid-19-shake-up-capitalism-11610817856.

Robinson Meyer, "A Legendary VC Has a Plan for Solving Climate Change," the *Atlantic*, December 8, 2021. https://www.theatlantic.com/science/archive/2021/12/legendary-vc-has-plan-solving-climate-change/620928.

Hamza Shaban, "Climate Change Is an Opportunity to Dramatically Reinvent the Economy," the *Atlantic*, September 19, 2014. https://www.theatlantic.com/business/archive/2014/09/

climate-change-is-an-opportunity-to-dramatically-reinvent-the-economy/380429.

Ruchir Sharma, "The Rescues Ruining Capitalism," *Wall Street Journal*, July 24, 2020. https://www.wsj.com/articles/the-rescues-ruining-capitalism-11595603720.

Alec Stapp, "What Many Progressives Misunderstand About Fighting Climate Change," the *Atlantic*, September 25, 2022. https://www.theatlantic.com/ideas/archive/2022/09/capitalism-clean-energy-technology-permitting/671545.

OPPOSING
VIEWPOINTS®
SERIES

CHAPTER 2

What Is Capitalism's Role in Society?

Chapter Preface

When did capitalism actually begin? The answer to what seems like a straightforward question depends a lot on who you ask and how you define "capitalism."

Capitalism's supporters tend to see the system as reflecting something central and intrinsic to human nature. The free market was a song that had been playing from the very start of civilization itself, a melody that has only grown louder with the passage of time. Through this lens, all attempts to reform capitalism could not operate outside of the boundaries created by the system. From this perspective, potential rival systems—such as Soviet communism—were essentially at odds with human nature, a flawed utopian ideal that was doomed to fail.

Unsurprisingly, those on the other side tended to think differently. They argue that it was capitalism that manipulated human nature and made it into something ugly. It was the pursuit of capital that stepped all over ideas of common decency and cooperation that felt central to the long-term idea of human survival. From this worldview, the larger problems are problems with the current system rather than humankind itself.

The perspectives in this chapter showcase a vigorous debate between these polarizing views of the world and how they manifest through issues like data collecting and running the world created by social media. They consider the question of whether a world without capitalism is possible and whether that would be a positive thing. The question itself—when and why capitalism came to represent the dominant form of organizing economies—remains largely unanswered in any particular sense. But the question provides a lens through which to examine capitalism's impact on the world as an organizing principle, both today and in the past.

> *"Proponents of socialism and social democracy would have you believe that capitalism is a purely Western construct."*

Capitalism Is Older than You Think

Dioné Harley

In this viewpoint, Dioné Harley asserts that the origins of capitalism date back over 2,000 years. Forget about Adam Smith; Harley is thinking about the writings of Xenophon, who documented the market practices of ancient Persia in the 4th and 5th centuries BCE. According to this viewpoint, Cyrus the Great was taught as a prince how to judge market transactions using ideas like property rights and consent, which in some people's eyes form the basis of free market thinking. According to this reading, the free market appeared whenever civilization seemed to be at hand and could be considered fundamental to human progress. Dioné Harley is a writer for the website Bbrief, which is an African-based content forum that provides access to the latest management information.

As you read, consider the following questions:

1. Why does Harley think that human beings are programmed to arrange themselves hierarchically?
2. What are "human status hierarchies?"

"Capitalism Is Not Recent or 'Western', It Is Natural and Necessary for Prosperity," by Dr Dioné Harley, Bbrief, December 15, 2020. Reprinted by permission.

3. How old does this author think capitalism really is?

Proponents of socialism and social democracy would have you believe that capitalism is a purely Western construct that carries no deeper legitimacy in terms of our evolutionary development or our historical roots.

They claim that the hierarchical nature of capitalism was imposed by the West, and without this system, humans wouldn't arrange themselves hierarchically. They also claim that capitalism as an economic system was developed in the West in the 18th century and was not practiced in the rest of the world before this time. Both these claims are incorrect.

Human Evolutionary Development

Socialists often claim that the hierarchical nature of capitalism has forced people to arrange society in ways we otherwise wouldn't, and these hierarchies are fundamentally oppressive, thereby casting capitalism purely as a tool for oppression.

In actual fact, human beings are programmed to arrange themselves hierarchically based on our evolutionary development. This arrangement is not forced on us, but naturally occurs no matter the context we find ourselves in.

It has been shown that infants and young children form, represent and coordinate within transitive hierarchies in adaptive ways from as young as nine months, and they do this because they assume that rank will lead to more resources.

What's important to note is that the nature of the hierarchy is not set in stone. The kind of hierarchy that comes into existence can vary, depending on the context and the participants.

Research by Lotte Thomsen of Oslo University shows that human status hierarchies don't only reflect formidability-based dominance but also consensual deference for legitimate authorities, leaders and competent and prestigious experts. These kinds of hierarchies can facilitate social coordination and serve as models for culturally transmitted learning, stimulating freely conferred respect.

In other words, even though capitalism has been depicted as fundamentally nefarious in virtue of its hierarchical nature, whether the hierarchy is destructive or constructive depends on how it is implemented—capitalism isn't necessarily oppressive in nature.

On the contrary, it is the only system that has reliably led, throughout history, to progress in terms of quality of life.

Origins of Capitalism

The claim that capitalism is a comparatively recent phenomenon borne only out of the West is also false because the starting point of capitalism as an economic system predates the thinking of Adam Smith—the philosopher and economist who is considered the father of capitalism. This calls into question the idea that capitalism is a purely Western tool of domination.

Xenophon's writings predated Smith by 2,000 years, and he documented the market practices of ancient Persia—an economy that made use of market mechanisms.

Xenophon also wrote about Cyrus the Great in 550 BC, Iran, who was taught as a prince how to judge market transactions on the basis of whether they were conducted in alignment with property rights and consent, which forms the basis of free market thinking.

Enterprises, banks, advanced commercial practices, and free markets can be traced 4,000 years back to countries we would now view as part of Syria. The development of these civilisations shows that markets have been fundamental to human progress all along.

Archaeologists have found many tablets from Babylonia and Assyria that are receipts of economic ventures. This reveals the economic activity of private profit-seeking merchants, sophisticated investment ventures, as well as market price setting. Diaries also show how these prices changed on a monthly, or even weekly, basis in Babylonia.

Historians have found enough evidence to suggest that the market economy was a Middle Eastern innovation.

Free markets, in one form or another, also formed in three cradles of human civilisation—India, China, and Mesoamerica. We know that China has continuously vacillated between free market policies and statist control, with the greatest progress taking place during its free-market periods.

Chinese thought was also captured in the *Guanzi*, a 7th century BC text that describes how profit-seeking merchants studied demand and supply in the marketplace. Confucius advocated for less taxation and Mencius argued that price setting shouldn't be influenced by the state, while private property should be protected —all features of free market thinking.

Prosperity Historically Linked with Capitalism

Europe only became technologically superior in recent times. Prior to Europe's adoption of modern capitalism, it was the Middle East, China, and India that were responsible for growth and technological innovation.

Even the Aztecs and Mayan people in Mesoamerica had economies with the features of a free market. What this shows is that prosperity has historically been linked with capitalism.

Evidently, capitalism has been misrepresented as a Western tool of oppression when it in fact aligns with our natural inclinations and predates the development of the West. If we are to conduct a fair and accurate critique of capitalism, then it doesn't serve us to attack a strawman.

| *"Most things that humans need or want tend to become commodities."*

Socialists Have Something to Say About Capitalism's Role in Society

Adam Buick

Unlike the author of the previous viewpoint, Adam Buick is less content with capitalism. The criticism of capitalism presented in this viewpoint comes from a socialist in the United Kingdom, who makes the case that the dehumanization implicit to capitalism reduces the quality of life of those who live under it. This argument relies, in some sense, on the old Marxist idea of alienation, which points to the space between people and the communities around them. By making everything about commerce, something in everyday human interaction is lost, Buick says. Buick is a socialist based in London, who has been called one of the "most active members" of the Socialist Party of Great Britain and is a contributor to the organization's Socialist Standard magazine.

As you read, consider the following questions:

1. What are "money-commodity relations?"
2. Why do socialists think that capitalism is not the most efficient way of providing for people's material needs?

"Capitalism and the Quality of Life," by Adam Buick, The Socialist Party of Great Britain, January 2006. https://www.worldsocialism.org/spgb/socialist-standard/2006/2000s/no-1217-january-2006/capitalism-and-quality-life/. Licensed under CC BY-ND 2.0.

3. What is the "different criticism of capitalism" that this
   viewpoint considers?

C apitalism is a society where nearly all the things that humans
need or want are articles of commerce, things made to be
bought and sold. This is not a complete definition since under
capitalism one thing in particular becomes a commodity—the
human ability to work and to create things, what Marx called "labour
power—and this is in fact the defining feature of capitalism. It's a
commodity society in which labour-power is a commodity.

This has two consequences. The first is that there is not simply
production for sale but production for profit. And secondly, most
things that humans need or want tend to become commodities, i.e.
have to be bought. It is not difficult to see why. The wages system
means that most people are dependent, for satisfying their needs, on
the money they are paid for the sale of the one saleable commodity
they do possess (their labour power), money which they then use
to buy what they must have to live. So the "commodification" of
labour power means the commodification of food, of clothes, of
accommodation, and of other, less material wants too.

One of the things that the spread of capitalism meant, in
concrete terms, was the spread of money-commodity relations.
It's a process that's still going on in parts of the world and which
even conventional economists speak of as integrating formerly
largely self-sufficient subsistence farmers in Asia, Africa and Latin
America into the "money economy."

What we are talking about here is the commodification
of people's *material* needs. Some people might not find this
objectionable. Some even find it a progressive, even a liberating
development. In fact this is one of the standard defences of
capitalism—that the money economy gives people the freedom
to choose what to consume by how they spend their money and
that this is the most efficient way of organising the satisfaction
of people's material needs and wants. Of course this isn't true in
that it assumes that the economy responds to consumer demand,

whereas in fact it responds to changes in the rate of profit, while most people's "demand" is limited by the size of their wage packet or salary cheque.

That capitalism is not the most efficient way of providing for people's material needs—and that socialism as a system of common ownership, democratic control and production just for use would do this much better—is the traditional socialist case against capitalism. And it retains all its validity. But, after the last World War, in the 50s and 60s capitalism in North America and Western Europe appeared to live up to its promise of material prosperity for most people through the emergence of the so-called "consumer society." But then another, different criticism of capitalism appeared: that while it might have solved more or less adequately the problem of "bread," of dire material want, for most people in these parts of the world, it had still not created a satisfactory society.

Books began to appear in America with such titles as *The Lonely Crowd*, *The Organization Man*, *The Hidden Persuaders*, *The Waste Makers*, *One-Dimensional Man*, all critical of various aspects of the "consumer society" as a society in which people were encouraged to regard the acquisition of more and more consumer goods as the main aim in life. In Europe, such criticism took on a more explicitly anti-capitalist form. In France the critical books bore such titles as *A Critique of Everyday Life* and the *Society of the Spectacle*. The argument was that in the "consumer society" (called instead, more accurately in fact, "commodity society") the logic of buying something to passively consume had spread from the purchase of material goods to other aspects of everyday life—to how people spent their leisure time and to how they related to each other.

This type of criticism added another dimension to the socialist case against capitalism: that it not only failed to organise the satisfaction of material needs properly but that it also degraded—dehumanised—the "quality of life."

It's not clear to whom the credit for developing this "cultural criticism" of capitalism should go. The Frankfurt School of Marxism (Fromm, Marcuse and others), the Situationists, even radical journalists in America like Vance Packard, would be among the candidates. In any event they were all working on the basis of the observable fact of the degrading effect capitalism was having on the *quality* of everyday life by spreading commercial values more and more widely.

It's a powerful criticism of capitalism. Perhaps even these days, in this part of the world, a more powerful criticism than the traditional socialist one that capitalism brings material poverty to most people. Certainly, on a world scale, there are hundreds of millions in dire material poverty. And there are few millions in this country—around 15 percent of the population—who are materially deprived. But we can't say this of the majority of the population here. Most people in Britain don't have a problem about getting three meals a day, decent clothes, heating, don't have to go to the pawnbrokers or live in vermin-invested rooms. In fact, the commodification of the "wants of the mind" is based on the fact that most people have money to spend on satisfying wants over and above those of "the stomach." If people didn't have this discretionary purchasing power after having satisfied their material needs, then there would be no market for cultural and entertainment products for capitalism to stimulate, manipulate and exploit. (As to why people have this "extra" money to spend on entertainment, it will have something to do with increased intensity and stress at work requiring more relaxation—more escapism—for people to recreate their particular ability to work.)

The criticism of "consumer society" was not just that it represented the invasion and colonisation of every aspect of social life by money-commodity relations, but that it also encouraged passive consumption rather than active participation. There is a great deal of validity in this point—that the "consumer society" is one where, sometimes literally, people sit in armchairs watching the passing show provided for them. This is a criticism of people's

WHAT IS ECONOMIC ANTHROPOLOGY?

Economic anthropologists study processes of production, circulation and consumption of different sorts of objects in social settings. 'Objects' includes material things, as well as what people do for each other (such as provide labour and services) and less visible objects (such as names, ideas and so forth). The settings range from small and intimate social units like households through intermediate ones, like firms, villages or local markets, to very large entities like regional systems of ceremonial exchange or global systems of advertising and consumption.

While the settings and processes that are studied vary tremendously, most economic anthropologists approach them in two main ways. One approach is concerned with social context: what sorts of people make, give, take or consume which sorts of things, and in what sorts of situations do they do so? In a sub-Saharan African village, who is it who tends food crops—men or women, old or young, married or single, and so forth? In England, which sorts of households are likely to have computers, and which household members are likely to use them? Another approach is concerned with cultural context: how do different sorts of people understand their economic activities, the objects involved and the people with whom they carry out those activities? When an artisan sells something to a buyer, how does each party think about their relationship and the objects that they exchange?

Thus, while economic anthropologists study economic processes, their approach is different from that of economists. Economists usually restrict themselves to monetary transactions and try to develop formal, abstract models of economic systems. Economic anthropologists, on the other hand, usually are concerned with all forms of production, circulation and consumption, monetary or not. Further, they are concerned less with developing formal models and more with trying to describe and understand economic actions in their social and cultural context.

"Economic Anthropology," by Dr. James G. Carrier, Royal Anthropological Institute.

lack of participation is shaping their lives, a lack that was also reflected politically where "democracy" is conceived of as merely choosing every four or five years between rival would-be elites (using in fact marketing techniques to attract support). Instead of people making their own sport or their own entertainment—or politics—they consume them as a pre-packaged commodity.

There must be something wrong with a society in which, instead of people living their own lives and interacting with their neighbours in a human way, they sit in front of a screen watching actors perform artificial scenes based on exaggerations of everyday life and identifying with the fictitious characters in these programmes. And in which the most widely-read newspapers don't discuss real events so much as the artificial ones portrayed in these programmes and the lives and loves of the leading actors who play in them—as well as those of other so-called "celebrities" from the world of sport and entertainment.

As long as capitalism lasts, the quality of life will continue to decline. There's nothing that can be done to stop this within the context of capitalism as it is due to capitalism, representing, as it does, the dissolving effects on society of the spread of money-commodity relations into all aspects of life. So, despite the slow, but undeniable increase in material living standards in certain parts of the world the case for socialism as a non-commercial society in which human welfare and human values will be the guiding principle retains all its relevance. With the common ownership of the means of life, there could and would be production directly to satisfy human needs and wants and not for sale with a view to profit—the death of the commodity, the end of what William Morris called "commercial society"—and a classless community with a genuinely common interest in which humans can relate to each other as human beings and not as social atoms colliding with each other on the market-place as commodity buyers and sellers.

> *"So much for 'technology' serving the interests of democratic movements."*

Techno-Capitalism Is Not the Answer

David Correia

In this viewpoint, David Correia expresses the disappointment he felt with media reports depicting the role technology played in the Arab Spring protests of the early 2010s. Ultimately, these products don't exist in an idealistic void, he writes, they are products that are bought and sold in a capitalist society with the intention of turning a profit. And in a capitalist society, capital is king, and as such technology should not be viewed as a source of moral or social good. The moral disappointment of capitalism should come as no surprise, according to Correia. David Correia is the writer and author of the book Properties of Violence: Law and Land Grant Struggle in Northern New Mexico.

As you read, consider the following questions:

1. Why does Correia say that most people ignore the cultural, political, and economic complexity of technological artifacts?
2. According to this viewpoint, what would a consideration of the role of technology in the unrest engulfing the Arab world look like?

"Democracy, Capitalism and Technology", by David Correia, CounterPunch, February 4, 2011. Reprinted by permission.

3. According to Correia, what's disappointing about
   how technology has been used during the Arab
   Spring protests?

A mong the many amazing images of social unrest that have
come out of Egypt over the course of the past week includes
a nighttime photo that depicted a group of young protestors
huddled in the middle of Tahrir Square huddled around a small
fire kindled from scrounged scraps of wood. The photo was used
widely by dozens of media outlets including *The Washington Post*,
The Daily Kos and *The Huffington Post*. What was most remarkable
about the photos was how it was displayed in the *New York Times*.
Throughout the past week, the *Times* has offered an incredible
slideshow of photos taken by photojournalists from the AP, Reuters
and the European Pressphoto Agency. The *Times* prominently
displayed the campfire photo as a remarkable depiction of disparate
protestors making common cause over the shared intimacy of a
simple campfire. It is a nearly universal image. We have all circled
around campfires, brought together by the warmth and light of the
fire, and in doing so have shared intimacies and forged social bonds.

What was most interesting about the photo, however, was the
way in which the *Times* chose to display it. The campfire photo
was immediately followed in the slideshow by another nighttime
photograph of Tahrir Square. Another shot of protestors huddled
in a circle together. Another photo of protestors sharing a brief
intimacy amid enormous chaos. But in this photo the light they
shared wasn't the light of a small kindling fire, but rather light
emitted from a pile of blinking cell phones recharging on a
communal extension cord.

The uncanny familiarity between the two photos illustrates a
central theme of so much of the coverage of the unrest in Tunisia
and Egypt over the past month: the central role of technology
and its role in producing democratic transformations via free
markets. According to the photo, the cell phone has replaced the
campfire as the hearth around which we build our most intimate

social relations. And the cell phone photograph, juxtaposed as it is against the campfire photo, suggests that while the source of social relations and intimacy (from stone age campfires to 21st century technology) may have changed the way in which we express those social relations has not. Cell phones are the new campfires and we owe our social bonds and most intimate relations to them.

This photo was the compelling visual representation of an ongoing trope among many commentators, journalists, and political activists. According to the *Times* and the *Guardian*, and debated on Democracy Now and in endless blog entries and Twitter feeds, the unrest we have been witnessing in Tunis and Egypt is the "Facebook" or "Twitter" revolution.

But this obsession with the technological essence of the unrest in the Arab world—is it, or isn't it the techno-revolution?—has unfortunately been marked by a profoundly uncritical debate over the role of technology in the political and economic convulsions we have been witnessing. Deeper investigations into the role of technology have been ignored in favor of the fetish of the Facebook. And this is nothing new. The fetish of Facebook and Twitter echoes the fascination with the technological innovations understood as inherent and progressive in capitalism. And because of it we have cell phone revolutions.

While some commentators have been quick to dismiss the absurd idea of a Facebook revolution, these interventions they have largely ignored the central way in which technology is understood: technology as an autonomous, independent agent of change—THE causative agent driving human progress. The ubiquitous objects of technology have finally become so much a part of everyday life that they have become invisible to critical scrutiny.

As a result many critics have responded to the banality of claims of technological progress at the heart of the Egyptian unrest with equally banal claims about the limits of technology. We are subjected to discussions of the political implications of technology that often slide into "he said, she said" absurdities.

While much of the punditry on the role of technology in the events unfolding in Egypt reveal the depth of truly shallow views of technology, the political and economic context of the uprising in Cairo offers, if anything, an antidote to claims of technological determinism and an opportunity to develop a critical view of technology that examines the political economy of technology.

First, (and perhaps the most obvious and most noted) Facebook and Twitter aren't "technology." They are commercial firms with services developed and deployed as commodities that circulate solely as a means to capture surplus value and thus provide a return on investment for shareholders.

Celebrations of technology, or out-of-hand rejection of technology, that rely on the simplified view of technology (Facebook = technology) not only ignore the political economy of technological development in capitalist society, not only valorize and reinforce the dangerous notion of an independent techno-authority, but by doing so foreclose the close scrutiny of technology and democracy in capitalist society. We ignore the cultural, political and economic complexity of technological artifacts and let off the hook the people, institution and worldviews that rely on these tools to reproduce inequality and injustice.

While many critics of the idea of a "Facebook revolution" have pointed out that the protests in Egypt have developed largely without the aid of Facebook or Twitter, this phenomenon has not been fully explored and does not go far enough.

A consideration of the role of technology in the unrest engulfing the Arab world should consider how particular political structures and economic arrangements have produced and relied on particular tools of oppression expressed through control of everyday objects of technology. Starting at this critical vantage point, instead of around the virtual campfire, takes us somewhere else entirely.

The events in the Arab world over the past two weeks have starkly revealed the authoritarian structures and reactionary politics embedded in nearly all of the objects and artifacts upon which we have come to rely on and refer to so innocuously as "technology."

First, the same US corporations heralded as the source of technology-driven revolution (Facebook and Twitter) are hardly the most important US technology corporations implicated in the unrest in Egypt. Narus, a California-based company founded in 1997 and owned by Boeing, developed and now sells what they call "real-time traffic intelligence" equipment to countries and corporate clients. Among their many clients are Egypt Telecom and the U.S. super-spies at the National Security Agency. Narus provides equipment that provides the capacity for on-the-spot surveillance of internet communications. NSA conducts these procedures on a daily basis in ongoing violation of the Foreign Intelligence Surveillance Act but at the continued pleasure of the White House. Mubarak, his hand ever on the handle of authoritarian tools delivered to him by his corporate friends, has used this capacity with a vengeance over the past week, targeting activists and interrupting communications. This hasn't been the "Facebook revolution." If anything it is the "Narus Revolution" brought to you by the friendly international team of trainers in the National Security Agency.

Second, Egypt not only conducts surveillance, but also literally controls access to digital information, demonstrated by their rapid digital response to social unrest. They shut down all internet traffic in Egypt because all internet traffic runs through one of four commercial ISPs. They were ordered to shut down and they complied. The internet is not the virtual commons, it operates as a virtual marketplace in the same way that the mall does—it is private property. It's infrastructure owned and controlled by corporations and governments on stand-by to protect their interests. As long as all you do is shop, you're fine.

Mubarak ordered UK-based Vodaphone to shut down mobile phone texting. This was easy, of course, because in order for Vodaphone to acquire a license to operate in Egypt it had to agree to conditions and government control and oversight.

They did so happily. Such is the logic of capitalism. So much for "technology" as an autonomous, independent agent of social change and democracy.

Senators Susan Collins of Maine and Joseph Lieberman of Connecticut have long been working on legislation to make Mubarak's malevolent tactics our federal law. Their bill would give to the President the authority to "declare a cybersecurity emergency," and "order the disconnection" of certain networks or Web sites. This authority would "not be subject to judicial review."

So much for "technology" serving the interests of democratic movements. In the end, the particular objects and artifacts of everyday "technology" are the tools of corporations and authoritarian governments. And by now it should be clear that democracy and capitalism do not cohere and the revolution cannot be carried out via "technology." Rather the struggle must become a struggle over the social, political and economic conditions that have made the everyday objects of technology—our digital campfires—nothing more than the tools of authoritarian despotism and capital accumulation.

And over the past few days, this is precisely what has happened in Egypt. The trite talk of techno-progressivism and techno-democracy has been silenced by scenes of bloody confrontation between Mubarak's reactionary goons and protestors no longer huddling around cell phone campfires. They are fighting in the streets as anti-Mubarak protestors are breaking up bricks ("the broken-brick revolution!?") to heave at knife-wielding pro-Mubarak attackers as they fight against a regime long propped up by its technological authoritarianism.

> *"The idea that the modern tech economy depends on two-way—not one-way—flows is often lost in the public debate about data usage."*

Bartering with Non-Monetary Flows

Gillian Tett

Websites often like to collect data about their users, and in this viewpoint the financial writer Gillian Tett says that she would rather people refer to this collecting as a kind of bartering. This is because that wording suggests there's something two-way about the transaction: users get to use a website for only the price of their Internet bill, and websites make money by selling ads that appear on those websites. But advertisers tend to believe that it's important to get the right ads in front of the right people, and they think the secret to knowing who future buyers are is located in the vast amount of data people emit when they click on things. Gillian Tett is a writer who, most recently, has run the editorial board at the Financial Times.

As you read, consider the following questions:

1. What does "barter" mean in the context of this viewpoint?
2. Does the two-way transaction between websites and users described in this viewpoint seem fair?

"The Data Economy Is a Barter Economy", by Gillian Tett, Harvard Business School Publishing, July 6, 2021. Reprinted by permission.

3. What fuels the "endless controversy" that Tett describes
   around selling data?

T he use of consumer data today is expanding exponentially
—as is public and political criticism of these practices. Just
think of the political scandals that exploded a couple of years ago
around Cambridge Analytica. Or regulators around the world
examining whether social media platforms such as Facebook have
abused their monopoly powers.

The new bipartisan bills calling for tighter tech regulation that
are now circulating in the U.S. Congress—and the appointment
of Lina Khan to head the Federal Trade Commission—will only
inflame this debate.

So, what is the best way for businesses to use data in a way that
feels ethical to consumers and does not spark a regulatory backlash?
This question is sparking endless angst in today's C-suites. All
manner of policy responses have been suggested: breaking up tech
giants, redefining monopoly controls, introducing new privacy
laws, and letting consumers "own" their data to name a few.

One simple and important place to start is to change the way
we talk about it. Policy makers, economists, techies, lawyers,
business leaders, and consumers should borrow an idea from
cultural anthropology and consider the concept of "barter." Doing
this will clarify the minds of regulators and investors to focus on
the scale and nature of long-concealed exchanges that now lie at
the heart of the tech world, and how to create a more acceptable
framework that protects consumers.

At first, this might sound odd. After all, anthropology is one
of the least-known social sciences—it's probably most famously
associated with Indiana Jones. And the word "barter" conjures
up images of swapping meat for berries—an image that seems
far removed from the modern C-suite, let alone Silicon Valley.

Economists tend to assume that barter is a prehistoric practice
that disappears whenever societies invent money—that, at least, was
the scornful view of Adam Smith, the 18th century intellectual, and

it has shaped economic thinking today. Most Western executives have absorbed a cultural assumption that because "money makes the world go round"—to cite the cliché—the most important things in an economy are measured in monetary units and/or organized with money. Transactions that happen without money (i.e. those which are "free") are thus downplayed and/or ignored.

Anthropologists, however, have a much broader vision of how the economy works. They look at how exchanges bind societies together in a broad sense and know that money-based exchanges are only one of the flows that bind us together. Systems of social credit, gifts, and barter matter too, even if they are rarely discussed in public and cannot be easily factored into an economic model.

Looking at what is hiding in plain sight—i.e. non-monetary flows—can help frame the modern digital economy. After all, what drives the business strategy of companies such as Facebook, Google, and numerous others, is partly an exchange that does not entail money: Consumer data is being collected in exchange for the provision of internet services, just as berries might be swapped for meat.

I would argue that "barter" is the best word to describe this exchange. And if this phrase was inserted into the language of the C-suite and policy making today, with a broader anthropological perspective, this could deliver several benefits. Most notably:

1. It Would Make Everyone Aware of Both Sides of the Transaction

The idea that the modern tech economy depends on two-way—not one-way—flows is often lost in the public debate about data usage. Consumers are not just giving up data (which they sometimes hate), they're also getting services in return (which they almost always like). Since they don't want to lose the latter, they continue to deal with social media sites, even amid political outcry.

2. It Illuminates the Point that Consumers Don't Seem to Want to Pay for These Transactions with Money

In recent years, tech companies, have offered internet users ways of "selling" their data for money, and paying for internet tools (with money). For example, in 2019, Facebook, created a "Study" app that paid users for access to their data for market research purposes. But consumer interest and uptake has been low. Maybe that reflects inertia. But I suspect it reflects the fact that digitization has made barter so efficient that Adam Smith's assumption about the evolution of societies is wrong.

3. It Draws Attention to Scale and Significance of These Transactions for the Wider Economy

At present, these flows tend to be excluded from economic measurements (such as gross domestic product data) and investors' models of company valuations. This is a big mistake: This barter trade needs to be acknowledged to get an accurate picture of how the economy really works, and what companies are worth.

4. It Could Help Policy Makers Understand Today's Corporate Monopoly Power

In recent decades, American regulators tended to assume that the best way to tell whether a corporate monopoly exists (or not) is whether consumer prices were high. Khan, the new head of the FTC, is among those who have argued that this approach is outdated, since companies are using monopoly powers even when prices are low. Talking about "barter" might help frame this more effectively.

5. It Would Make It Easier to Build a Data System that Feels More Ethical to Consumers

The current system is provoking endless controversy. This isn't necessarily because consumers want to abolish the use of barter; they probably do not, given how efficient it is. What is needed, however, is an effort to change the terms of the barter trade to give consumers more power. How? By forcing companies to provide far more transparency in these trades and letting consumers control the duration of a trade (i.e. how long data is retained). Most important of all, consumers should be free to cut barter deals with different providers to create competition—which means that regulators should put the onus on tech companies to provide easy data portability, just as financial regulators put the onus on banks to make it easy for consumers to change bank accounts.

By acknowledging the word "barter"—and talking about what is hidden in plain sight—the private sector could and should reshape the current debate itself, embracing a broader vision of how our data economy works. Instead of talking about this in terms of a negative (i.e. "free" or the absence of money), we need a positive, active term.

Or, if you prefer, ponder another cultural wrinkle that economists and techies also often ignore: the original linguistic root of the word "data," which comes from the Latin word *dare*, meaning "to give." This might seem surprising in our modern numbers-obsessed world. Or maybe not: that original root meaning is a small reminder of the exchanges that bind us together, with far more than just money. We ignore this at our peril today. Think of that when you next toss that "data" word around.

> "Capitalism is changing, that is certain. But it is doing so in a way that has accepted, and is willing to commercially exploit, changing public sentiment concerning climate and change social inequalities."

The Environmental, Social, and Governance Framework Isn't Destroying Capitalism, It Is Just Changing How We Think About It

Carl Rhodes

In this viewpoint, Carl Rhodes discusses the increasing popularization of the environmental, social, and governance framework (commonly known as ESG) among corporations, which shifts focus away from just maximizing profits to considering the effects corporations have on society and the environment. According to its critics, ESG is a move toward corporate socialism, but Rhode argues that it is compatible with today's understanding of capitalism, which focuses on stakeholders in addition to shareholders. Today, consumers and shareholders alike are more critical of how corporations impact society, so it is in the best interest of corporations to act accordingly in order to thrive. However, Rhodes argues that companies who embrace the ESG framework do not go far enough to create a more equitable society. Carl Rhodes is a professor of organization studies at the University of Technology Sydney in Australia.

"No, BlackRock Is Not Leading a Marxist Assault on Capitalism," by Carl Rhodes, The Conversation, April 5, 2023. https://theconversation.com/no-blackrock-is-not-leading-a-marxist-assault-on-capitalism-203042. Licensed under CC BY-ND 4.0 International.

As you read, consider the following viewpoints:

1. According to Rhodes, who do ESG opponents consider to be central to the plan?
2. According to this viewpoint, how far back does the concept of corporate responsibility to society go?
3. According to Rhodes, what has caused the Marxist and socialist rhetoric in the conversation around ESG?

Five years ago it would have been unimaginable, but today there is a global movement convinced the world's largest corporations are engaging in stealth warfare to transform liberal democracies into neo-communist dictatorships.

At the heart of this corporate-led Marxist revolution, apparently, is the trend towards businesses not just focusing on profit maximisation but taking into account environmental, social and governance responsibilities (called ESG for short).

According to ESG opponents this is putting democracy on a downhill road to socialism—or worse.

Purportedly central to this sinister plan is United States company BlackRock and its chief executive, Larry Fink. BlackRock is the world's biggest funds manager, overseeing more than US$10 trillion in investments on behalf of clients such as superannuation funds. Fink is paid more than US$30 million a year, and his wealth is estimated to be more than US$1 billion.

You might think this would make Fink a very unlikely champion of destroying capitalism. But due to his support for ESG—particularly for business taking action on climate change —he's been accused of advancing a form of "corporate socialism", with ESG criticised as "socialism in sheep's clothing".

All the Way to the President

Concerns about the "woke" politics of ESG don't just live in the dark recesses of the internet. In the US it has become a mainstream fixation. Anti-ESG opinions abound in the pages of *The Wall Street*

Journal and on the infotainment network Fox News. It is a hot battlefield in the culture wars.

In 2020, the Trump administration proposed a rule requiring pension funds to put "economic interests" ahead of "non-pecuniary" concerns—in other words, to force them to ignore issues of long-term social and environmental sustainability and focus on short-term profits.

The Biden administration reversed this plan. But last month the US Congress passed a bill to reverse that reversal, with support from two Democrats in the Senate. Biden then used his presidential power to veto the bill—the first veto of his presidency.

In all likelihood ESG will be a major campaign issue in the 2024 presidential election. The speaker of the Republican-majority House of Representatives, Kevin McCarthy, has accused Biden of wanting "Wall Street to use your hard-earned money to fund a far-left political agenda." Republican presidential contender and Florida governor Ron DeSantis has also been railing hard against the "woke ESG financial scam."

A Short History of Stakeholder Capitalism

What's notable about all these emotive denunciations of ESG is that they demonstrate little understanding of how capitalism works.

This point was made by Fink in his 2022 annual letter to the chief executives of the companies in which BlackRock has invested clients' money.

> In today's globally interconnected world, a company must create value for and be valued by its full range of stakeholders in order to deliver long-term value for its shareholders. It is through effective stakeholder capitalism that capital is efficiently allocated, companies achieve durable profitability, and value is created and sustained over the long-term. Make no mistake, the fair pursuit of profit is still what animates markets; and long-term profitability is the measure by which markets will ultimately determine your company's success.

The idea that business owners have responsibilities to wider society is not new. It dates back at least to the 17th century when the modern corporate form began to emerge through innovations such as joint-stock ownership and the legal privilege of limited liability.

The origins of the corporate social responsibility and ethical investment movements can also be traced back hundreds of years —generally to groups and individuals motivated by religious values —and have been mainstream business ideas for decades.

Why? Because paying attention to social and environmental sustainability, ESG advocates argue, produces better long-term investment returns. If it didn't, businesses wouldn't be interested.

Arguing over the Best Way to Do Capitalism

This is not to say the application of ESG principles isn't above criticism—for going too far, or not going far enough—being mere window-dressing for the status quo.

But such arguments are over the best way to do capitalism. It's all about as far from interest in a neo-Marxist insurgency as can be imagined. Debating the best way to produce shareholder value has nothing to do with wanting a "revolutionary dictatorship of the proletariat" and to see private property abolished—key features of Marxism.

Capitalism is changing, that is certain. But it is doing so in a way that has accepted, and is willing to commercially exploit, changing public sentiment concerning climate and change social inequalities.

This is what businesses that make money do. They listen to customers, and other stakeholders—their workers, suppliers, the communities in which they operate, and the governments that regulate them. They plan for the future. They mitigate future risks.

Impoverishing Democracy

So what explains this fantastical rhetoric about ESG being the road to Marxist tyranny? In my view, it shows just how much the intellectual foundations of conservatism and liberalism have been debased in a media marketplace that favours reactionary emotionalism over tempered thought.

Economic conservatism (rooted in the belief in free markets, globalisation and small government) has become disconnected from social and political conservatism (especially as related to climate activism, social justice and diversity and inclusion).

All of this is a fatal distraction from the broader political and economic problems we face both locally and globally. It pushes serious discussions—such as what to do about economic inequality, political polarisation and declining social capital—into the background.

There are biting criticisms to be made about ESG that don't make the headlines. You don't often hear business-friendly ESG supporters campaigning for increases to the minimum wage, progressive taxation, worker solidarity or the need to curb the runaway train of executive compensation. Climate and social justice are pressing issues, to be sure. But they shouldn't push fair economic distribution and shared prosperity off the agenda.

Ironically, the bogus labelling of ESG as a Marxist plot also helps do this. It serves the interests of the very elites populist pundits and politicians claim they oppose. It works against the interests of the working-class people they claim they care about. That is not socialism.

Periodical and Internet Sources Bibliography

The following articles have been selected to supplement the diverse views presented in this chapter.

David Brooks, "I Was Once a Socialist. Then I Saw How It Worked," the *New York Times*, December 5, 2019. https://www.nytimes.com/2019/12/05/opinion/socialism-capitalism.html.

Caleb Crain, "Is Capitalism a Threat to Democracy?" *New Yorker*, May 7, 2018. https://www.newyorker.com/magazine/2018/05/14/is-capitalism-a-threat-to-democracy.

Nancy Fraser, "How Capitalism Worms Its Way into Every Aspect of Our Lives," *Jacobin*, December 8, 2022. https://jacobin.com/2022/12/dig-nancy-fraser-capitalism-social-reproduction-race-gender.

Daniel Immerwahr, "Beyond the State," the *Nation*, September 20, 2021. https://www.thenation.com/article/society/graeber-wengrow-dawn-of-everything.

Zachary Karabell, "Capitalism Doesn't Have to Be This Way," the *Atlantic*, May 21, 2021. https://www.theatlantic.com/ideas/archive/2021/05/brown-brothers-harriman-capitalism-public-service/618946.

James Mackintosh, "Quarterly Capitalism Isn't Ruining the World," *Wall Street Journal*, April 6, 2022. https://www.wsj.com/articles/quarterly-capitalism-isnt-ruining-the-world-11649237479.

Jerome Roos, "Capitalism Causes Disasters, Socialism Can Solve Them," *Jacobin*, April 5, 2020. https://jacobin.com/2020/04/coronavirus-capitalism-disasters-socialism-economic-collapse.

Jennifer Schuessler, "What If Everything You Learned About Human History Is Wrong?" *New York Times*, October 31, 2021. https://www.nytimes.com/2021/10/31/arts/dawn-of-everything-graeber-wengrow.html.

Ilana E. Strauss, "The Myth of the Barter Economy," the *Atlantic*, February 26, 2016, https://www.theatlantic.com/business/archive/2016/02/barter-society-myth/471051.

Jason Zweig, "Disturbing New Facts About American Capitalism," *Wall Street Journal*, March 3, 2017. https://www.wsj.com/articles/BL-MBB-58378.

CHAPTER 3

Are There Any Modern Alternatives to Capitalism?

Chapter Preface

As long as capitalism has existed, it has had critics, and those critics have imagined ways to replace the system with something else. In fact, for much of the recent history of capitalism, the system has been haunted by the specter of its supposed future; a socialist state predicted by the German writer and political philosopher Karl Marx (1818–1883) and his supports in the mid-1800s. Under the political philosophy of Marxist socialist theory, socialism would serve as a transitional state after capitalism is overthrown and before communism is fully enacted. According to Marx, communism would involve all property being publicly owned and the end of private property, social hierarchy, and even state power. Considering that this is diametrically opposed to capitalism, transitioning to the less rigid system of socialism—which still allows for money, private property, and a democratic government—seemed like the logical first step.

It would be a little while longer before a revolution would sweep such an idea—at least superficially—into power, but that eventually happened in 1917 during the Russian Revolution, when Russia became the Soviet Union (USSR). Following a long civil war, a self-consciously "communist" government took over the country and, from there, embarked on a nearly century-long effort to enact an economic system outside of the definitions of merchant capitalism. Instead of being run by the owners of the capital they used, businesses in these communist countries were owned by the state.

On a smaller scale, the political philosophy of democratic socialism has started to become increasingly popular in the U.S. over the past couple of decades due to politicians like Bernie Sanders and Alexandria Ocasio-Cortez. Under the form of democratic socialism that is becoming popularized in the U.S., capitalism would still play a major role in society, but there would be more social welfare programs in place to allow for a more equitable society. In this sense, it is much less revolutionary than the form of communism proposed by the Soviet Union in that it isn't intended to overthrow capitalism or any other political system, but find a way to make it fairer for the people living within it.

But outside of the dichotomy of socialism and communism versus capitalism, other alternatives have presented themselves. Inside capitalism, there were movements to use the power of capital to do things beyond dictate quick profits. There were businesses that were started as worker cooperatives and gave long-term employees the chance to rise up the ranks to central leadership. Over the last decade, the idea of mutual aid campaigns emerged and suggested a different way to organize aid efforts outside of the top-down dictates othat were so codified by the structures of capitalism.

The perspectives in this chapter look at all of these ideas, from the history that informs them to the ways in which they are trying to change today's economic, political, and social systems.

> *"What a sorry state of affairs to have to admit that the human species' short-sightedness, greed, and intent on amassing heaps of money, even if it means it is at the cost of the very condition of our continued existence —nature—have brought us to the brink of societal collapse."*

Capitalism Needs to Be Reset

Bert Olivier

In this viewpoint written in April 2020, the writer Bert Olivier uses the COVID-19 pandemic as a chance to dive into the works of another writer named David Harvey, who wrote a book called The Enigma of Capital and the Crises of Capitalism *in 2010. In his reading, Harvey anticipates the pandemic to come, when he wrote that "some ultimate limit" would eventually be reached in capitalist society. According to Olivier, the pandemic was exactly the kind of limit that Harvey had in mind, and it would be a good idea for society to take a long, hard look at how its systems failed to respond to the strain created by the pandemic and hope they can be recreated into something new this time. Bert Olivier currently serves as an honorary professor in the philosophy department at the University of the Free State in South Africa.*

"Covid-19 pandemic: An opportunity to press the reset button on capitalism?" by Bert Olivier, Mail & Guardian Online, April 27, 2020. Reprinted by permission.

As you read, consider the following questions:

1. Why does this viewpoint say that the pandemic presented structural problems that did not exist before?
2. Is Olivier optimistic about the chances that humanity will "come to its senses?"
3. How does Olivier characterize the urgency of using the pandemic as a moment to replace capitalism?

If ever there were a golden opportunity for humankind to press the proverbial reset button regarding the unsustainable way in which we live, it is now, in the midst of the global coronavirus crisis. The pandemic has brought economies worldwide to a virtual standstill and, in the process, given us clear skies and a glimpse of what the planet would be like without our species. And, regrettably, it appears—from numerous videos and news reports—that the world and its (other) creatures would be better off without us. Just this morning someone sent me a picture of a group of cats, in which one stood on its hind legs and told the rest: "They were called 'people' and they walked like this!"

That just about says it all. What a sorry state of affairs to have to admit that the human species' short-sightedness, greed, and intent on amassing heaps of money, even if it means it is at the cost of the very condition of our continued existence—nature— have brought us to the brink of societal collapse. Many scientists —like this one—have stressed that it is humans' "intrusion in nature" that has generated the transfer of the novel coronavirus to our species, and that—unless humans backed off—it would happen again.

In 2010 David Harvey, an authority on Marxist studies, wrote about the limits nature poses for capitalist expansion in his book, *The Enigma of Capital and the Crises of Capitalism*. He did so in the wake of the 2008 financial crisis, and then already he remarked that: "… there is a wide-ranging field of concern, of political anxiety and endeavour, that focuses on the idea of a crisis in the relation to nature, as a sustainable source of raw materials, as mere land for further capitalist (urban and agricultural) development, as well as a sink for an increasing stream of toxic waste."

A little further on, his words assume an almost prophetic tone: "There may be an imminent crisis in our relation to nature that will require widespread adaptations (cultural and social, as well as technical) if this barrier is to be successfully circumvented, at least for a time, within the framework of endless capital accumulation. The fact that capitalism has, in the past, successfully navigated around natural barriers, and that it has often done so profitably since environmental technologies have long been big business and can certainly become much bigger ... does not mean that the nature question can never constitute some ultimate limit."

I would wager that the novel coronavirus constitutes an incontrovertible sign that such a limit has been reached. I know exactly how supporters of capitalism—including Big Pharma—would react: "It's just a matter of finding a vaccine, and we'll be on our way again!" And I would respond: "Read what virologists and other medical authorities have stated, time and again, that the difficulties posed by this coronavirus for the development of a vaccine are indicative of problems further down the line, because already—compared to its viral predecessors, like the SARS and MERS viruses—it has presented structural problems that did not exist before."

The point is: the evolution of such viruses will not stop here. Difficult as it is to tame the coronavirus, the next one may prove to be even more evasive, because—as Charles Darwin taught us —everything evolves to overcome threats in its environment, and viruses are no exception.

Here, too, Harvey seems to have been prophetic regarding the probable emergence of the new pathogen that has paralysed the dominant economic system: "What we call the natural world is not some passive entity but, as the philosopher Alfred North Whitehead once put it, 'a system in perpetual search of novelty'. To begin with, tectonic movements beneath the Earth's surface generate instabilities that give us earthquakes, volcanic eruptions, tsunamis and other events, while instabilities in atmospheric and oceanic circulations give us hurricanes, tornadoes, snow storms, droughts and heat waves that have all manner of human consequences, albeit unevenly distributed, both geographically and socially. Furthermore, trading upon and profiting from human disasters induced by natural events is far too frequent a feature of capitalism to be taken lightly.

"While human action has successfully eliminated the bubonic plague and smallpox, it now has to confront entirely new pathogens and diseases such as HIV/Aids, SARS, the West Nile virus, Ebola and avian flu, to say nothing of the potential for a new mutated influenza pandemic of the sort that killed millions back in 1918. Climates have long been subjected to a whole range of forces that uncomfortably mix together human-induced and non-human elements in such a way as to make it difficult to determine which is which, even when the very best scientific minds are collectively put to work to figure out the global climatic consequences of human action. While the effects are indisputable, the full range of consequences is almost impossible to determine."

In the light of all of this, what are the chances for humanity to come to its senses and ditch the disastrous capitalist system for something better—whatever one might call that—something that would factor our indissoluble relationship with nature into economic relations? Even without having read Harvey, I would not be optimistic. People are fundamentally too attached to entrenched habits and customs (even bad ones: witness, patriarchy) to let go of these, even if their continued existence depends on it. Already companies the world over are champing at the bit to get going again, although I must add that some seem to have taken the lesson of the coronavirus seriously, up to a point—for instance, some airlines have announced seating and disinfectant regimen changes that would make it safer to fly.

COVID-19 CHALLENGES CAPITALISM

Covid-19 disease is subject to two mathematical properties. The first is the transmission coefficient, which under normal human-to-human contact conditions is greater than 2.0, with a doubling time of only a few days, similar in principle to an uncontrolled nuclear reaction. The second is the incubation period, usually two weeks, so that if a strict separation is maintained between people for at least this period of time, the transmission coefficient is reduced and the epidemic can be mitigated or suppressed.

Thus, the cost of delay in applying strict measures is counted by the number of infected and dead in the first wave, by the spatter of positive cases throughout the landscape, and by the risk of secondary or tertiary outbreaks if there do not remain strong controls passed the first wave.

The poor performance of the United States in this crisis was due to a combination of factors, all of them related to the diminishing competition of the public authority. The American ex ante system was effectively adapted to the conditions of an individualized and unequal society, but fragile, uncoordinated, and inadequate to face a common threat. Free market ideology and conservative social doctrine have underpinned this system and obscured its vulnerability to the point of suppressing scientific evidence and political efforts to maintain a common defensive capacity.

"COVID-19 and Capitalism," by Galbraith, James K., The University of Texas.

Critical Thinking Is Required

In 2010 Harvey was not optimistic about fundamental change, with good reason, which hinges on the inability of institutions such as universities to integrate truly critical thinking into the courses on offer. The reason? Universities are in the ideological grip of the hegemonic economic system (which has the political system over a barrel), and will, therefore, not allow truly critical thinking to seep into economics and accounting courses. Harvey insists that it is "… only when these critical ideas [are] carried over into the fields of institutional arrangements, organisational forms, production systems, social relations, technologies and relations to nature that the world would truly change."

Furthermore, as far as universities go, Harvey has more to add: "The repression of critical and radical currents of thought—or, to be more exact, the corralling of radicalism within the bounds of multiculturalism and cultural choice—creates a lamentable situation within the academy and beyond, no different in principle to having to ask the bankers who made the mess [in 2008] to clean it up with exactly the same tools as they used to get into it."

This may not seem to pertain to the coronavirus crisis, but it certainly does insofar as capitalism is at the basis of the encroachment on nature—need I remind anyone of the utterly stupid eradication of the world's foreststo plant palm trees for palm oil, and to make way for soya-bean production? This is what has affected the habitat of wild animals which, because they are placed under stress, are more likely to shed the viruses they carry and infect humans. Hence, and I shall not mince my words here: capitalism is the enemy—not only of poor people, but of all people, as well as other living creatures. Here is a lengthy excerpt from Harvey, in which he pulls no punches (take note, university administrators, if you have the guts to do what is right and just):

"But the current crop of academicians, intellectuals and experts in the social sciences and humanities are, by and large, ill-equipped to undertake such a collective task. Few seem predisposed to engage in that self-critical reflection that Robert Samuelson urged upon them. Universities continue to promote the same useless courses on neoclassical economic or rational-choice political theory as if nothing has happened and the vaunted business schools simply add a course or two on business ethics or how to make money out of other people's bankruptcies. After all, the crisis arose out of human greed and there is nothing that can be done about that!

"The current knowledge structure is clearly dysfunctional and equally clearly illegitimate. The only hope is that a new generation of perceptive students (in the broad sense of all those who seek to know the world) will clearly see that it is so and insist upon changing it. This happened in the 1960s. At various other critical points in history, student-inspired movements, recognising the disjunction between what is happening in the world and what they are being taught and fed by the media, were prepared to do something about it. There are signs, from Tehran to Athens and on many European university campuses of such a movement. How the new generation of students in China will act must surely be of deep concern in the corridors of political power in Beijing.

"A youthful, student-led revolutionary movement, with all of its evident uncertainties and problems, is a necessary but not sufficient condition to produce that revolution in mental conceptions that can lead us to a more rational solution to the current problems of endless growth. The first lesson it must learn is that an ethical, non-exploitative and socially just capitalism that redounds to the benefit of all is impossible. It contradicts the very nature of what capital is about."

As far as a generation of critically thinking—and importantly, critically acting—students is concerned, I am happy to say that I have always taught my students, from undergraduate to doctoral level, of capitalism's injustices (after all, as Socrates taught me, philosophy serves the truth, and not any ideological system), and several of them have become highly articulate critics of this deplorable system. Moreover, their very way of living testifies to their deep understanding of capitalism's depravity, and of its cultivation of greed in people, not least students in business schools and economic faculties at universities.

The time for such a critical student generation to advocate for the urgency of a transition to a life-promoting economic system has never been better than now, when the coronavirus has brought our world, and its problems, so clearly in focus.

> "We did not fully appreciate at that time that Gorbachev, unlike his predecessors, was fully aware of the depths that the Soviet economy had fallen."

The Collapse of the Soviet Union Shows the Weaknesses of Communism

Ty Cobb

In this viewpoint, Ty Cobb discusses the collapse of the Soviet Union in 1991, one of the major historical events in the long history of capitalism over the last century. Cobb looks at the country's fall from the perspective of a victor, referencing the ambitious post-capitalist goals that had formed the basis of the so-called communist "experiment." Through this frame, Cobb doesn't land on a single factor behind the system's implosion, but points to an endless siege that took the form of everything from intelligence and economic support for the Solidarity movement in Poland to convincing Saudi Arabia to flood the world with cheap petroleum in 1986. Ty Cobb is a lawyer who once served as an assistant U.S. attorney in Maryland and later worked for the Trump administration.

As you read, consider the following questions:

1. Who does this viewpoint say was responsible for the collapse of the Soviet Union?
2. Why did Mikhail Gorbachev think he had to put a brake on the U.S.'s increased military build-up?
3. Does Ty Cobb credit Ronald Reagan's diplomacy with Gorbachev with the eventual collapse of the country?

Marxist-Leninist doctrine predicted that capitalism would collapse on the "ash heap of history" as global communism triumphed as an economic system. Instead, 20 years ago last Sunday it was the vanguard of the international communist movement, the Soviet Union, which disintegrated.

The two individuals who played the most prominent roles in bringing about the end of the USSR were President Ronald Reagan and Soviet General Secretary Mikhail Gorbachev. The policies formulated and implemented by both had very different objectives in mind, but the end result was the same.

Beyond Détente: Promoting Fundamental Change in the Soviet System

Early in the Reagan administration a fierce fight had erupted regarding the wisdom of engaging the Soviet Union. Many conservatives were convinced that détente had shown that any attempt at negotiations or engaging Moscow was doomed to failure. They also tended to believe that the USSR was on the ascendancy, particularly in the global arena, witness the success of Moscow's backing for "National Liberation Movements" in Africa, Southwest Asia, and Central America. They leaned toward the sense that the regime, albeit aging, was firmly in control in Moscow and that any real change seemed impossible.

I was asked in 1981 by the National Security Council, through the then Military Assistant, ADM John Poindexter, to prepare a series of point papers on the state of the USSR and what US policy initiatives might be considered. I had just completed a 2-year IREX fellowship, which brought me to the USSR off and on the past two years.

My view was: The Soviet leadership was aging, the economy was in difficult straights (my dissertation was on the Soviet economy/energy dilemma), and the U.S. could pressure the USSR to achieve political and military change. Not sure how much impact the memos had, but they fed into the cauldron of competing opinions erupting within the Administration.

President Reagan was opposed to détente, but open to negotiating with the Soviets. This would come, in his mind, only after he had reversed the American military decline, resuscitated the economy, and restored confidence within the U.S. body politic. By 1983 he felt that we should reconsider our stance of not engaging the Soviets, based on what he perceived to be further Soviet decline and U.S. restoration of power and confidence. Yes, the 1984 elections and Nancy's prodding had a role in his thinking, but he was also buffeted in the other direction continually by the naysayers.

Reagan's policies were laid out in 1983 in NSDD–75, titled "U.S. Relations with the USSR." The document directed two core objectives: first, "to contain and over time reverse Soviet expansionism," and second, "to promote the process of change in the Soviet Union toward a more pluralistic political and economic system."

The directive also laid out specific goals: In Eastern Europe, loosening Moscow's hold on the region; with respect to Afghanistan, it was to "keep maximum pressure on Moscow . . . and ensure that the Soviets' political and military costs remained high" while the occupation continued.

NSDD-75 was a very ambitious strategic guide, one that overtly would attempt to "change" the Communist system by ending the Party's monopoly on power and bringing about the weakening of the Soviet economy. The directive called for a more ambitious media penetration (RFE, Radio Liberty) into the USSR and its vassal states, assistance to groups in the Soviet empire who would topple the Communist regimes, and use of our technological and economic leverage (e.g., to stop the Soviet gas pipeline to Europe).

Reagan and Gorbachev: One Wanted to Reform the Soviet System; the Other to Fundamentally Change It

For Reagan the immediate goal was to insure that the Soviets bore the burden for actions they were taking to support anti-Western political movements and for pouring a considerable portion of their national wealth into the defense-industrial sector. For Gorbachev, who came to power in 1985 after years of desultory "leadership" behind aging and infirm General Secretaries–Brezhnev, Andropov and Chernenko–the objective was to reform a stagnating economic system through restructuring ("perestroika") and greater openness ("glasnost").

We did not fully appreciate at that time that Gorbachev, unlike his predecessors, was fully aware of the depths that the Soviet economy had fallen. It also appears that Gorbachev was deeply concerned about the President's SDI program ("Star Wars"), believing that what was at stake was more than just a space defense program. He believed that if the United States once and for all combined its technological superiority with its economic potential, America would make an enormous "skachok" (leap) ahead. The General Secretary knew that he needed to redirect resources away from the defense sector to rejuvenate the stagnating Soviet economic system, but first he must stop the U.S. potential to jump ahead—which he feared our pursuing SDI would do.

To do that he had to put a brake on Reagan's military build-up. He also realized that deep and fundamental reforms of the corrupt, centrally managed political system needed to be undertaken. While he recognized that this would cause some disruption, he failed to anticipate that the changes he was implementing would soon spiral out of control.

Reagan was not content to allow events to proceed in the USSR on Gorbachev's timetable. The United States took several measures to impose a burden on Moscow if it chose to continue its aggressive support of national liberation movements, its domination over East Europe, and its extensive funding of the military. Reagan directed that the U.S. support resistance movements against the Soviets in Central America and Africa, provide advanced missiles (e.g., Stingers) to the Mujahideen in Afghanistan, and support revolutionary movements in East Europe.

Specifically, working closely with Pope John Paul II (not well known even today!), the U.S. provided intelligence and economic support for the Solidarity movement in Poland that led to the first crack in the Soviet Empire. Reagan also secured support from Lane Kirkland, head of the AFL-CIO, which provided key assistance to Solidarity.

America also persuaded its friends to assist in these efforts, including encouraging Saudi Arabia to "turn on the oil spigot" and flood the world with cheap petroleum in 1986. This act severely undermined the Soviets' primary means to secure hard currency, depleted its foreign exchange reserves, made it difficult for the Soviets to import badly needed grain, and deeply impacted the thinking of the Soviet leadership.

By 1986 the war in Afghanistan led to increased public discontent, the Chernobyl nuclear plant disaster seemed to personify the regime's ossification and inability to handle crises, and the economy declined in the face of bad harvests and low global oil prices. Glasnost had led to the appearance of more popular media outlets, which then proceeded to highlight corruption in the highest echelons, rampant alcoholism, what the Stalinist regime had really done to the populace, and other formerly taboo topics.

The Empire Crumbles: 1989-91

James Mann argues persuasively that Ronald Reagan defied the advice of his more hard line advisers and skillfully led the negotiations with Mikhail Gorbachev that led to the fall of the

Soviet Union ("The Rebellion of Ronald Reagan"). I would agree. In fact, the President was constantly told by his chief intelligence experts, principally then Deputy Director of the CIA, Bob Gates, most Pentagon officials, and many State Department experts, that the General Secretary was not seeking fundamental change of the Soviet system and that at any rate it remained strong and impervious to outside leverage. Reagan disagreed and on many occasions overruled his advisors and directed that we engage the Soviet leadership in negotiations while continuing to exert pressure on the USSR's economy. I believe that history has shown Reagan to be right in the course he chose.

By 1989 Moscow was faced with increasing challenges. Afghanistan was clearly a failure, and the regime agreed to withdraw Soviet forces that year. Confronted with large street demonstrations in East Europe against the puppet regimes, Gorbachev and Foreign Minister Shevardnadze refused repeated pleas from their Warsaw pact allies to intervene militarily—as they had done in Hungary in 1956 and Czechoslovakia in 1968. As a result the Berlin Wall tumbled down, Germany was reunited, and Solidarity assumed power in Poland and Vaclev Havel's "Velvet revolution" succeeded in Prague. And in 1991, following a failed coup attempt, the USSR itself dissolved.

In the end, the combination of greater political and social freedoms instituted by Gorbachev and the proactive policies implemented under Reagan to impose severe economic and political burdens on Moscow together led to the collapse of the Soviet Union, on Christmas Day, 1991.

> *"State control of every aspect of the economy became the new gospel."*

The Failure of Socialism in Africa

Takudzwa Hillary Chiwanza

This viewpoint by Takudzwa Hillary Chiwanza surveys the legacy of socialism among countries in post-colonial Africa, where he says that following a non-explicitly Western economic model appealed to many. But the author is of the opinion that these efforts largely failed because of endemic political corruption, which created domestic economies that were unable to satisfy the needs of a growing, rapidly industrializing population. As one example, Chiwanza points to the leadership of Ghana under Kwame Nkrumah, where Chiwanza says that about 4 out of the 64 state-run enterprises were profitable by the time a military coup brought Nkrumah's leadership of the country to an end. Takudzwa Hillary Chiwanza is a writer and lawyer based in Zimbabwe.

As you read, consider the following questions:

1. Why was African socialism seen as a middle ground between Western capitalism and Soviet communism?
2. According to Chiwanza, how many countries in Africa ended up adopting socialist economic systems?

"Here Is Why Socialism Failed in Africa," by Takudzwa Hillary Chiwanza, The African Exponent, July 27, 2020. Reprinted by permission.

3. Why does Chiwanza think that the USSR's socialist model was "fundamentally flawed?"

The emergence and development of socialism in Africa came as a result of finding a new rallying point to foster economic growth in Africa. African nationalism had already united people together for the independence cause and African socialism stood as the new ideology for economic prosperity. It was a middle ground between Western capitalism and Soviet communism (the latter which adopted socialism for the administration of the whole Soviet Union). But as time progressed, the inefficiencies and loopholes of socialism in Africa got apparent and it was clear that the intended purposes of the ideology had failed to usher in comprehensive economic success for the continent.

As several African countries got their independence in the 1950s and 60s, the rejection of capitalism grew in popularity. Colonialism had brought capitalism and its evils to the continent. The rejection of capitalism at that time was a natural reaction by African leaders and a way to garner wide public support. It was lauded as a viable alternative regarding the economic prosperity of the continent. Between 1950 and the mid-1980s, 35 countries in Africa had adopted socialism in various forms. The wave of independence that swept across the continent at that time was supposed to empower the continent with true economic liberation, but this was not to be the case as the leaders dismally failed at executing their noble ideas.

The main inspiration for African socialism obviously came from the Union of the Soviet Socialists Republic (USSR, later Russia) and with how rapid industrialization was taking place in the USSR, there was a proven track record that socialism premised on the pre-colonial African society would work. The socialist running of the USSR also served as an inspiration for African countries because it was a departure from the capitalist machinations of the West. The way that the USSR was catching up with the United States of America and other European economic powerhouses compelled African leaders to think that they could also rival these Western superpowers.

It was also imperative for African countries to rapidly industrialize and modernize their infrastructure. State control of every aspect of the economy became the new gospel. But what was not understood was that the model from the USSR was fundamentally flawed because of egregious corruption and state force. The commanding nature of doing things was disastrous. In as much as the African countries claimed that their socialism was based on the precolonial traditions, the commanding nature of doing this made the implementation of the ideas futile.

Some of the main proponents of the socialist principle in Africa included Kwame Nkrumah of Ghana, Julius Nyerere of Tanzania, Leopold Senghor of Senegal, Ahmed Sekou Toure of Guinea, Kenneth Kaunda of Zambia, among others. For these leaders, African socialism promoted the ideals of togetherness as one community, as opposed to the individualistic nature of capitalism. African societies place emphasis on the role of the community, and as such, socialism was deemed a natural alignment with this. On the other hand, socialism provided an excuse for these leaders to trample on any dissenting opinions, effectively muzzling the opposition. The liberal ideals of democracy, which were an offshoot of capitalism were eschewed.

In the countries that chose socialism, the State emerged as the owner of the means of production. The economy had to be controlled by the State. Kwame Nkrumah introduced the Seven-Year Development Plan in 1964 which was heavily influenced by socialism. Private businesses were taken over by the State, leading to the birth of numerous state enterprises. Private capital was essentially abolished. Price controls were instituted such that by 1970, there were nearly 6,000 price controls relating to more than 700 product groups. Tanzania's 1967 Arusha Declaration was the basis for a socialist state (Ujamaa). Workers and peasants were intended to own and control the means of production. Private capital was nationalized, and this included banks, insurance companies, and foreign trading companies.

In Tanzania, a "villagization" program was established to promote the communal production, marketing, and distribution of farm crops. Emphasis was placed on the community values that existed in precolonial African societies. Peasants were moved to new co-operative villages under resettlement programs which commenced in 1973. These new government villages were the idealized socialist way of running the whole agricultural process —from production to distribution. All crops were to be bought and distributed by the government as it was illegal for peasants to sell their own yield.

Ethiopia also did the same thing as there were forced resettlements on government farms. The idea was to harness the power of the community through collectivized agriculture. Mozambique also sought to establish a socialist state with collectivized agriculture, crop growing schemes, and village political committees. The concept of villagization as adopted in various countries was intended to increase food and cash crop production. Everyone was supposed to be included in the economic processes of the country. Common facilities for farming were intended to be availed to everyone capable of producing agricultural yield. The universal provision of social services such as education and health was supposed to be the hallmark point of African socialism.

In countries that embraced socialism, it meant that the state was at the helm of the economy. All the power was vested with the state. Governments became increasingly authoritarian because of such accumulated and consolidated power. All unoccupied land was appropriated by the governments. Marketing boards were tightened to ensure that they ripped off the producers, especially the farmers. Price controls peaked excessively.

This was the situation in Guinea under Sekou Toure as reported by *The New York Times:* "Unauthorized trading became a crime. Police roadblocks were set up around the country to control internal trade. The state set up a monopoly on foreign trade and smuggling became punishable by death. Currency trafficking was punishable by 15 to 20 years in prison. Many farms were collectivized. Food prices were fixed at low levels. Private farmers were forced to deliver annual harvest quotas to 'Local Revolutionary Powers.' State Companies monopolized industrial production."

Despite the good ideals propounded by African socialism, that the whole society must own and control the means of production, the concept was an abysmal failure and led to widespread poverty. State controls led to artificial shortages and black markets became rampant. State-owned enterprises simply could not deliver. Most of these were inefficiently operated and were massively unprofitable. When Nkrumah was toppled from power, about 4 of the 64 enterprises were profitable. The bureaucracy of these enterprises resulted in appalling levels of corruption. This was detrimental to the interests of the whole economy at large. When people attempted to challenge these failures, they were met with brute force from the state. Many were sent to imprison, and some were executed. Force and terror were the means of communication that these African governments understood.

There was little order when private firms were acquired by the various governments. The result was utter mismanagement as there was no defined methodology to run these enterprises. For example, the "Ghana government-owned sugar factory at Komenda, after completion, stood idle for more than a year because it lacked a water supply system." There was little incentive for proper management of these enterprises. Another example is the Ajaokuta Steel Mill in Nigeria. The Nigerian government purchased a steel-making furnace in 1975 manufactured by the Russians but it was built on a site distant from iron and coal mines such that it was rendered useless. Up to now, despite many capital injections, the factory is still useless yet over 100,000 people were on the payroll drawing pension.

The shortages which came as a result of state controls promoted rent-seeking activities. People wanted to increase their wealth without creating any new wealth. Illegal enrichment became the order of the day. Import and exchange controls became the most profitable activities. Ministers would demand a commission before issuing out import licenses. Some governments would deny import licenses to import newsprint to newspapers that were critical of them. People would buy scarce commodities at government-controlled prices so that they could resell those commodities on the black market for an enormous profit. The leaders who were at the forefront of socialism were the same ones who raided their countries' treasuries and deposited such monies into private accounts in foreign banks.

African socialism failed to outlive the USSR. The fall of the USSR in 1991 killed any form of socialism that had existed as an official government policy in African countries. The force of democracy pushed by the West tore into the USSR, and that same force found its way in Africa too. Multi-party elections became the norm in several African countries. The death of the USSR was also the final death of socialism in Africa. The USSR had been run on communist ideology, although the State was administered in a purported socialist manner. The USSR was focusing on heavily militarizing the state such that collective farming had declined sharply. The same behavior was also manifested in African countries that adopted socialism.

Socialism in Africa failed because the leaders wanted to rapidly industrialize without paying attention to the peculiarities of their own countries. It failed because in trying to achieve mass ownership of the means of production and eradicate classes and class struggle, the leaders were selfish, corrupt, and used terror to enforce their ideas. There was no regard to the economic realities of the day. Everything was done haphazardly to garner mass support. It would however be prudent in this day to incorporate some of these ideas and mix them with the neo-liberal capitalist principles that dominate African economies today in order to reduce income inequalities among the citizens.

> "The flexible structure encourages all community members to contribute their ideas and skills to meet their unique needs."

Mutual Aid Is Solidarity

Victoria Méndez

In this viewpoint, Victoria Méndez writes about a newer alternative to capitalist power structures: the idea of mutual aid, which grew in popularity amidst a number of recent catastrophes like Hurricane Maria in 2017 and, later, the COVID-19 pandemic. But this perspective draws on the longer history of collective aid efforts, which Méndez sees as a direct precursor to these more contemporary efforts. Méndez argues that this way of thinking about communities allows aid efforts to reflect the unique needs of the communities they are a part of. Victoria Mendez is an associate with the disaster response team at GlobalGiving, a Washington, DC-based nonprofit that organizes donations.

As you read, consider the following questions:

1. What does mutual aid mean, according to this viewpoint?
2. How far back, historically, does the writer of this viewpoint pinpoint the beginning of the idea of mutual aid?

"What Is Mutual Aid, And How Can It Transform Our World?" by Victoria Méndez, GlobalGiving, February 3, 2022. Reprinted by permission.

3. What about the idea of mutual aid makes it appear flexible to its supporters?

Growing up, I watched my parents translate government documents and job applications for neighbors. After Hurricane Maria, I watched in awe as my 80-year-old Abuela cleaned Puerto Rico's debris-filled streets with a machete. Dozens of our neighbors joined her, and they cleared all the roads by the end of the week.

These experiences and countless others showed me that community and service are inseparably linked. The idea is nothing new. For centuries, mutual assistance networks have supported many Indigenous, Black, LGBTQIA+, immigrant, and low-income communities' survival and access to essential services.

What Does Mutual Aid Mean?

Mutual aid is about cooperating to serve community members. Mutual aid creates networks of care and generosity to meet the immediate needs of our neighbors. It also addresses the root causes of challenges we face and demands transformative change.

Amid an unrelenting pandemic, economic crisis, and increasing climate disasters, the need for mutual aid networks has grown significantly. These crises expose the deeply rooted systemic inequalities in our society—including in humanitarian aid. And mutual aid has always played a role in filling those gaps.

Imagine Water Works, a mutual aid organization focused on climate and social justice in Louisiana, is one example.

"As we navigate several crises at once, they [mutual aid networks] are models of the world that we're trying to build together," Imagine Water Works Executive Director Klie Kliebert said.

Here are three reasons why mutual aid is a powerful tool for change:

1. Mutual Aid Is Not New

Mutual aid in the form of collective self-reliance has existed for ages. Today, Indigenous families rely on long-established kinships and traditions to support entire communities. These traditions emphasize relationships and interconnectedness between oneself, communities, ancestors, future generations, and the earth. They're critical to one another's wellbeing and are often reflected in cultural practices and teachings.

For example, our partner Instituto Chaikuni used Indigenous knowledge and ancestral healing techniques during the COVID-19 pandemic in underserved Indigenous communities in the Amazon. It showcases how Indigenous peoples paved the way to protect communities and promote collective wellbeing—and continue to do so.

Mutual aid also has roots in political and activist communities around the world. In the late 1700s, recently freed African Americans were still denied access to banks and social safety nets. So, they pooled money to buy farms and land, care for children, the sick, and the entire community.

As Chinese immigration to the United States increased in the 19th century, mutual aid societies, or huiguan, formed to represent and protect the people from different regions and dialect groups. These societies influenced the lives of many Chinese immigrants by providing temporary housing, financial assistance, and support in finding employment. They also became a means of speaking out against rising anti-Chinese sentiment.

In the 1950s, Native Americans developed community centers to protect native resources and advocate for Indigenous rights after the government terminated the recognition of more than 100 tribes.

A decade later, organizations like the Black Panther Party and the Young Lords leveraged mutual aid to expose racial inequities by building care and resource distribution centers through their community survival and free breakfast programs. These efforts helped shape modern-day mutual aid. Today, the framework has grown in popularity as an essential form of COVID-19 relief and has become central to the battle against systemic racism. Mutual aid must be part of the equation to eliminate barriers for groups that have been historically discriminated against.

2. Mutual Aid Is Solidarity

It can take many forms. The flexible structure encourages all community members to contribute their ideas and skills to meet their unique needs. What helps build that sense of solidarity is a mutual understanding of how a pandemic, economic crisis, and climate disaster affect all of us, explained Janet MacGillivray, founder of Seeding Sovereignty, an Indigenous-led collective network. In the wake of the pandemic, Janet witnessed firsthand how Indigenous communities bore the brunt of the effects.

In response, Seeding Sovereignty mobilized an Indigenous Impact Community Care Initiative with the Apache, Navajo, and dozens of Pueblo nations to provide relief to Indigenous communities across New Mexico and other parts of the United States.

"We share a common goal of serving our communities in whatever ways are needed—from distributing personal protective equipment (PPE) and free food to sending Indigenous-authored books to families in quarantine," Janet said.

Mutual aid networks don't require community members to fill out burdensome paperwork or require anything in return for their support. This helps reduce the stress, stigma, and shame sometimes associated with asking for help.

3. Mutual Aid Respects Unique Needs

Community, compassion, and respect are the core of mutual aid work. At the height of the pandemic, Imagine Water Works launched the Trans Clippers Project after receiving requests for a haircut.

"At first, some team members questioned the urgency, but as a trans person, I understand that it's more than just hair—it's an expression of their gender identity," Klie explained.

"We intend to create a shame-free community, in which folks can ask for what they need without fear of judgment. I don't have to understand your request to respect you."

Imagine Water Works quickly responded, and within months, the Trans Clipper Project became a global movement, providing hundreds of transgender, nonbinary, and two-spirit people with hair clippers.

"This is the kind of creative, community-led, and inspired work that's possible when you lead from a place of kindness and curiosity, as opposed to shame and fear," Klie said.

| "Democratic socialism is a political philosophy in which ordinary people have a real say in their workplaces and the economy as a whole."

This Time, Socialism Can Be Democratic

Samuel Arnold

In this viewpoint, written by Samuel Arnold in the year of the 2020 presidential election, the author takes a broad look at a surge in support for socialism in the years since Bernie Sanders' 2016 presidential run. In particular, he is interested in the idea of democratic socialism, which he explains in detail as a mechanism to give ordinary people a real say in their workplaces and the economy as a whole. Looking at the power that mega-companies like Amazon wield in the country, Arnold suspects that ideas like this appeal to people concerned with making a more democratic society. Samuel Arnold is an associate professor who teaches political theory at Texas Christian University.

As you read, consider the following questions:

1. According to this viewpoint, how popular is socialism among Americans ages 18 to 29?
2. What groups generally "side with Trump in rejecting socialism?"

"What Is Democratic Socialism and Why Is It So Popular?" by Samuel Arnold, Teen Vogue, May 1, 2020. Reprinted by permission

3. What is democratic socialism, compared to
    ordinary socialism?

S ocialism: it's back. Left for dead after the Cold War, revived
by Bernie Sanders's 2016 and 2020 presidential bids,
and popularized by social media superstars like Representative
Alexandria Ocasio-Cortez (D-NY), the concept has gone
mainstream. According to a 2018 Gallup survey, 51% of
Americans age 18-29 have a positive opinion of socialism, as
do 57% of Democrats. And the COVID-19 pandemic lent new
urgency to discussions about creating a more fair and equitable
economic system.

Of course, not everyone's a fan. Count former President Donald
Trump among the holdouts.

"Here, in the United States," Trump declared in his 2019 State
of the Union address, "we are alarmed by the new calls to adopt
socialism.... Tonight, we renew our resolve that America will never
be a socialist country."

Many Americans side with Trump in rejecting socialism.
Despite its increasing popularity among younger Americans and
Democrats, socialism remains broadly disliked, especially by
Republicans and seniors.

So who's right? That's for you to decide. But first you need to
know some basics. What *is* socialism, anyway? Coming up with
one all-encompassing definition of socialism throughout the ages is
impossible. But here's some background on what modern socialists
in the United States are discussing and arguing for.

What Is Democratic Socialism vs. Socialism?

Democratic socialism is a political philosophy in which ordinary
people have a real say in their workplaces and the economy as
a whole.

Let's use Amazon as an example. Jeff Bezos, Amazon's founder
and CEO, is really rich. Like, $120 billion rich. Bezos's money

doesn't just buy him fancy stuff, such as his new $165 million Beverly Hills mansion; it also gives him real power.

Ask yourself: Who controls the American economy? Who calls the economic shots? Ordinary working people, or wealthy capitalists like Bezos? The answer is the latter. Under capitalism, key economic decisions are made not by all members of society but by the very richest members — those wealthy businesspeople who own what Marxists call the "means of production."

Consider Amazon's recent decision to build a second headquarters. This was a big opportunity for cities across the country; winning Amazon's "HQ2" would potentially mean 50,000 new jobs and $5 billion in local investment.

It's no surprise that over 200 cities submitted bids, each scrambling to assemble the most business-friendly package of tax cuts and other perks. Amazon eventually awarded HQ2 to northern Virginia, an already prosperous area. The fact that other regions, like Detroit, stood in greater need of economic development didn't matter.

From the socialist perspective, this example perfectly illustrates capitalism's core flaw: its profoundly undemocratic nature. Under capitalism, we don't make economic decisions collectively. We don't decide together where 50,000 new jobs should be created, or $5 billion in capital should be invested.

Instead, rich capitalists like Bezos can do what they like with the means of production. After all, it's their property.

Socialism — in its modern, democratic form — aims to turn this picture on its head. Rather than allowing a tiny elite to call all the economic shots, modern socialism wants to empower ordinary people to make these decisions collectively. Under democratic socialism, major industries and large corporations would be brought under social ownership and control.

Would the state then own everything? No, for two reasons.

First, democratic socialism targets only the economy's "commanding heights" — think Walmart and other Fortune 500 corporations — not smaller-scale productive properties like your local pizza place. Nor does socialism have any beef with personal property: Socialists don't want to collectivize your toothbrush, your iPhone, or your Nintendo Switch.

Second, democratic socialists seek "public" or "social" ownership of the economy, which is not necessarily the same thing as "state" ownership. Although state ownership is certainly an important mechanism in the democratic socialist tool kit, it's definitely not the only one.

As American socialist Michael Harrington puts it, social ownership means "the democratization of decision making in the everyday economy;" it's a "principle of empowering people at the base, which can animate a whole range of measures" beyond state ownership — "some of which we do not yet even imagine."

It's in this "empower the base" spirit that democratic socialists have proposed measures that have nothing to do with state ownership, per se. These include measures like: "workplace democracy," which gives workers rather than bosses control of their workplaces; "participatory budgeting", which empowers ordinary citizens to direct their city's spending, e.g., on parks rather than prisons; and "universal basic income," which, by giving each person a no-strings-attached check each month, increases everyone's "real freedom" to pursue what really matters to them.

To modern socialists, then, socialism means "economic democracy." Across the globe, 18th- and 19th-century radicals overthrew monarchs like the United Kingdom's King George III, replacing political dictatorship with political democracy. Socialists say that we should complete what these revolutionaries started; we should dispossess our *economic* monarchs like Jeff Bezos, thereby replacing what many view as economic dictatorship with economic democracy.

What Democratic Socialism Isn't

This definition of socialism as economic democracy will surprise many people. It is at odds with three popular but deeply mistaken ways of understanding modern democratic socialism.

The first confuses democratic socialism with statism; it says that socialism just means state control of the economy, even if the state in question is profoundly undemocratic. This view regards dictatorships like the Soviet Union, Venezuela, and North Korea as socialist, precisely because they achieved total state control over the economy. But many would argue that these examples are not at all socialist; contemporary socialists believe that socialism requires robust political and economic democracy — the very antithesis of these authoritarian regimes.

A second mistaken conception of democratic socialism conflates socialism with social democracy; it says that countries like Denmark and Sweden, which tax citizens heavily and spend generously on social programs like unemployment insurance, education, and health care, are socialist. (Arguably, this is the conception of socialism advanced by Bernie Sanders, who, when pressed to explain what he means by socialism, tends to refer to northern European countries with ample social spending supported by high levels of taxation.) But socialism isn't, at root, about taxation or social spending; it's about who controls the means of production. You can't prove that a country is socialist by referring to its tax rate or unemployment benefits.

That said, at least one of the Nordic countries — Norway — probably *does* deserve to be called socialist. Again, this is not because of its taxing or spending, but because of its ownership profile: According to an analysis from the People's Policy Project, the Norwegian state (which is highly democratic) owns over 60% of national wealth, and over 76% of national non-home wealth.

A third mistaken conception of democratic socialism assumes that socialism must oppose not merely private ownership of the means of production, but also markets and profits. Under this conception, socialism seeks to replace *market production for profit* (e.g., Walmart makes socks in order to make money) with *planned production for use* (e.g., government planners tell the sock factory to make socks because people need them).

Admittedly, most socialists in the past, especially those in the Marxist tradition, did conceive of socialism in this anti-market way. But many contemporary socialists, influenced by the economic and moral failures of centrally planned economies like the Soviet Union's, tend to accept some role for markets and profit seeking in their socialist visions. What they call "market socialism" attempts to combine the economic democracy of socialism with the most functional parts of capitalism.

Arguments Against Socialism

Socialism has attracted fierce and wide-ranging criticism. Below are some of the more important objections.

First, thinkers like Nobel-prize-winning economist Milton Friedman have argued that socialism is incompatible with political freedom. They say it's incredibly dangerous to concentrate economic power in the hands of the state. State ownership of the economy leads, inevitably, to political tyranny. Just witness the atrocities committed by socialist states like the Soviet Union, Vietnam, and North Korea. (Of course, socialists do not agree that these are actually socialist states; see above.)

Second, economists argue that anti-market forms of socialism — those that rely on planners rather than the profit motive to direct production — are sluggish, inefficient, and bad for innovation. Planning leads to bread lines; markets lead to Tesla and smartphones. (Socialists will point out that this objection does not apply to market-friendly forms of socialism.)

Third, some philosophers argue that socialism's emphasis on economic equality is misguided. Economic inequalities are not in themselves objectionable. Provided that everyone has *enough*, who cares if some have more than others? As long as capitalism gives everyone a decent standard of living, we shouldn't worry about its tendency to create vast economic gaps, or so these philosophers contend.

Fourth, some philosophers argue that economic democracy is not actually desirable. Democracy, whether political or economic, is risky. Uninformed participation can make things worse. Do we really want ordinary workers controlling the economy? On this line of thought, they assert, perhaps it's better to leave important decisions to experts.

Arguments for Democratic Socialism

Socialists have offered many arguments for socialism. Here are some of the most important.

First, they argue that socialism is much more democratic than capitalism. It empowers ordinary people, not just rich owners, to make economic decisions.

Second, socialism would harness our collective wealth to meet everyone's basic needs, or so its advocates maintain. No longer would some people be fantastically rich while others are reduced to begging in the street. Key needs like food, shelter, health care, education (including college), and retirement support would be "decommodified" — provided to all, regardless of ability to pay.

Third, supporters argue that socialism would greatly reduce the stark inequalities of income that we find in capitalist countries like the United States, where CEOs are compensated at up to 278 times the rate of average workers, as one recent Economic Policy Institute study found. In the Mondragón cooperatives in Spain, which are owned and controlled by their workers, the ratio between highest- and lowest-paid is closer to 5:1.

Fourth, socialists argue that their economic system would eliminate the massive wealth inequalities found in capitalist countries. Under capitalism, the economy's commanding heights are owned by a small elite. Under socialism, ownership of major means of production would be dispersed and democratized, or so advocates contend. The result, socialists claim, is a radically egalitarian, classless economy — an economy in which everyone is an owner.

Finally, socialists argue that by relaxing (if not completely eliminating) the demands of profit-driven economic competition, socialism opens space for a more cooperative, humane, less alienating economy that treats workers as people rather than disposable inputs.

> *"The economic system almost all of us participate in everyday (willingly or not), barely has 50% of people that support its continued existence."*

Half of Americans Want a Viable Alternative to Capitalism

Drew Serres

In this viewpoint originally published on OrganizingChange.org, Drew Serres explains the findings of surveys indicating that 50 percent of Americans are unhappy with the capitalist system. He asserts that people-powered movements such as the Occupy Movement in 2011 can pressure governments and financial systems to adjust to meet the American public's interests. Serres also argues that there are a number of different alternatives to capitalism as it currently exists, including business and worker cooperatives, restructuring corporations, moving to smaller-scale banking, and moving to values-based economic analysis. Drew Serres is the creator and writer of the Organizing Change blog.

As you read, consider the following questions:

1. What data does Serres cite in this viewpoint?
2. What examples does Serres give of business cooperatives?
3. What are the "Big Four" banks in the U.S.?

I used to think I only knew a few people besides myself who truly desired a system beyond capitalism. I used to think folks would just disregard me if I clearly stated my anti-capitalist views.

Well it looks like our "radical" views to implement alternatives to the current expression of capitalism are almost the majority opinion.

In the last few years, the Pew Center and even the right-leaning Rasmussen Reports found estimate that around 50% of the U.S. population wants to do away with our capitalist system.

Just think about that for second.

The economic system almost all of us participate in everyday (willingly or not), barely has 50% of people that support its continued existence.

While this has not trickled up to our governmental or financial systems yet, our people-powered movements have shown the anger many feel at our corporatized economy (e.g. in our medical and higher education systems) and the passion they have to create alternatives (e.g. increasingly impactful Evergreen Cooperatives of Cleveland).

While the Occupy Movement has gained the most attention since its prolific spread across the U.S. and world, what may be just as important is the paradigm shift that has led a near majority to desire something other than capitalism!

Next time you are walking down the street, just consider the fact that every other person you see is seeking a new economic system that puts our values front-and-center. I know thinking about this definitely gives me motivation!

So let's look at how exactly we can disrupt capitalism and craft a system that focuses on meeting the world's needs (and not just the needs of the few).

What Are Some Alternatives to the Current Expression of Capitalism?

Now that it's clear frustration with capitalism is reaching new heights, we have to be consciously thinking of how to channel that energy into shaping a new livable, people-centered, and sustainable economy.

So what are some of the key ways changemakers are showing us how we can, at this very moment, be pushing forward a monumental shift away from hierarchical capitalism?

These examples listed below may still participate in the current economic system, but often do so in dramatically different ways that demonstrate alternatives are entirely feasible.

Business cooperatives and worker cooperatives—where workers collectively own and manage the business

As I mentioned earlier in this post, the Mondragon co-op system in Spain with 85,000 members and the Evergreen Cooperatives of Cleveland are perfect examples of robust business that also propel forward our other values (e.g. sustainability and ethical practices).

These systems are already having a noticeable positive economic impact and that trend only looks to grow.

There are many different types of cooperatives including: Mesh Networks (i.e. internet co-ops), Community Land Trusts, health care collectives, bike shares, utility cooperatives, artists collectives, and so many more!

Restructuring corporations—e.g. corporate rechartering and ending corporate personhood

Right now our current corporate law actively reduces ethical business practices. This is due to the fact that, right now, corporate charters include only an interest for *shareholders*, but they should also include interest for *stakeholders*.

Another big push to change corporations is by ending "corporate personhood" (i.e. idea that corporations should have the same legal status/protection as people). Move to Amend, a national network of organizations and individuals, is leading this charge for ensuring corporations remain accountable economic justice and to all people.

Smaller-scale banking—i.e. moving our capital away from huge banks, and instead investing in small scale banks and city/regional/state banks

You might have heard a bit of criticism of Big Banks (i.e. the "Big Four" in the U.S. of Bank of America, Citigroup, JPMorgan Chase, Wells Fargo) in recent years, and much of that is due to the Big Banks' inability to support communities and small-businesses after the crash they created.

These banks are too large to be responsive to local dynamics, so there is an increasing call for small-scale banks.

These smaller scale banks can take the form of regional, state, or even city-owned banks. Currently the only state-owned bank in the U.S. is the Bank of North Dakota, which has been a keystone to North Dakota's ability to withstand the financial crisis.

Moving to a values-based economic analysis— shifting beyond GDP to a system that incorporates the needs and aspirations of our society

GDP per capita (gross domestic product) is the dominant means for measuring a country's standard of living; however, this lens of the world obscures what people actually seek in life (e.g. health, happiness, and leisure time) or even promotes long-term detrimental actions (e.g. strip mining and deforestation).

Though there has been no wide-spread adoption of alternatives to GDP per capita (other than the pathmaking country of Bhutan), there are an increasing number of groups calling for new systems. Some examples include the Genuine Progress Indicator (GPI) used in Maryland, and the UN sponsored indicators of World Happiness.

What Does a Majority Seeking Alternatives to Capitalism Mean?

It means showing people a vision of a world based on expressing human values and potential, instead of one based on never-ending growth.

The examples above show that this movement is growing. The dedicated efforts prove a more holistic approach to social betterment is already here.

I now know we're already halfway there, now let's keep building a new infrastructure to support the other 50%!

Periodical and Internet Sources Bibliography

The following articles have been selected to supplement the diverse views presented in this chapter.

Maggie Astor, "Are You a Democratic Socialist?," *New York Times*, September 22, 2018. https://www.nytimes.com/interactive/2018/09/22/us/politics/what-is-democratic-socialism.html.

Greg Ip, "Two Capitalists Worry About Capitalism's Future," *Wall Street Journal*, April 24, 2019. https://www.wsj.com/articles/two-capitalists-worry-about-capitalisms-future-11556110982.

Casey Michel, "The Failed Dream of Mikhail Gorbachev," the *New Republic*, August 31, 2022. https://newrepublic.com/article/167602/mikhail-gorbachev-death-russia-legacy.

Jesse Norman, "How Adam Smith Would Fix Capitalism," *Financial Times*, June 22, 2018. https://www.ft.com/content/6795a1a0-7476-11e8-b6ad-3823e4384287.

Allison Schrager, "America's MBAs Are the Latest Skeptics of Capitalism," *Bloomberg*, June 28, 2022. https://www.bloomberg.com/opinion/articles/2022-06-28/america-s-mbas-are-the-latest-skeptics-of-capitalism?..

Cole Sinanian, "'Mutual Aid' Is a Radical Ideal. Some Live Its Communal Spirit," *Christian Science Monitor*, January 30, 2023. https://www.csmonitor.com/Business/2023/0130/Mutual-aid-is-a-radical-ideal.-Some-live-its-communal-spirit.

Noah Smith, "The Choice Isn't Between Capitalism or Socialism," *Bloomberg*, July 23, 2019. https://www.bloomberg.com/opinion/articles/2019-07-23/the-choice-isn-t-between-capitalism-or-socialism?.

Farah Stockman, "'Yes, I'm Running as a Socialist.' Why Candidates Are Embracing the Label in 2018," *New York Times*, April 20, 2018. https://www.nytimes.com/2018/04/20/us/dsa-socialism-candidates-midterms.html.

Gillian Tett, "Does Capitalism Need Saving from Itself?," *Financial Times*, September 6, 2019. https://www.ft.com/content/b35342fe-cda4-11e9-99a4-b5ded7a7fe3f.

Benjamin Wallace-Wells, "The Marxist Who Antagonizes Liberals and the Left," *New Yorker,* August 31, 2022. https://www.newyorker.com/news/annals-of-inquiry/the-marxist-who-antagonizes-liberals-and-the-left.

Martin Wolf, "Why Rigged Capitalism Is Damaging Liberal democracy," *Financial Times*, September 18, 2019. https://www.ft.com/content/5a8ab27e-d470-11e9-8367-807ebd53ab77.

CHAPTER 4

Is Capitalism a Force for Moral Good?

Chapter Preface

In this final chapter, we look at the question of whether or not capitalism is a source of any moral value. On one hand, most value systems look down on the idea of greed, considered by some a foundational element in the logic of capitalism. On the other, capitalist societies have generated massive wealth. Sometimes, some of that wealth goes toward helping people and supporting causes.

Central to that latter idea is the giving economy. In capitalist societies, charity acts as the private, redistributive element that is meant to move money from those with large amounts of it toward those who need it. The biggest charities are the projects of some of the biggest capitalists. The Bill and Melinda Gates Foundation, for instance, at one point donated more to the World Health Organization than any group or country except for the United States.

Critics, however, say this gives the people who possess these vast amounts of money too much power. Unlike governments, which are also charged with taking care of the people who live in a society, charitable organizations are not exactly accountable to anyone besides their donors. Often, those donors prefer to move their money through those kinds of foundations because they want to stay hidden. Sometimes these charitable groups end up becoming major donors to political campaigns and become ways for moving money from private hands to politicians under the cover of a respected cause.

The viewpoints in this chapter take a careful look at these questions. They showcase a debate that's at the center of the promise of capitalism. Is it a system that is responsible for generating the resources needed for an advanced and modern world? Or is the system of a giving economy fundamentally flawed? What should be considered a moral virtue when it comes to economic systems? Capitalism and the giving economy pose these very questions.

> "To be sure, some people see charity as a religious or moral obligation that they must try to uphold regardless of their personal economic circumstances. But for some of us, giving is a luxury rather than a necessity that can go on hold when times get tough."

Giving Decreases in the Wake of the COVID-19 Pandemic

Patrick Rooney and Jon Bergdoll

This viewpoint by Patrick Rooney and Jon Bergdoll looks at how the charitable giving economy changed at the beginning of the COVID-19 pandemic, taking a somewhat pessimistic view of the steady role those organizations have to play in keeping an equitable society afloat. In moments of economic downturn, giving tends to decline, despite the increased needs that those moments create, write Rooney and Bergdoll. Another thing they notice about times of precarity is that the bulwark of the giving world is "inherently limited" compared to the power of something like a government stimulus package. Patrick Rooney is an economist at the Indiana University Lilly Family School of Philanthropy and Jon Bergdoll works as a philanthropy statistician.

"What Happens to Charitable Giving When the Economy Falters?" by Patrick Rooney and Jon Bergdoll, The Conversation, March 23, 2020. https://theconversation.com/what-happens-to-charitable-giving-when-the-economy-falters-133903. Licensed under CC BY ND 4.0.

As you read, consider the following questions:

1. What is the correlation between charitable giving and economic downturns, according to this viewpoint?
2. How do the authors see the role of charitable foundations in the giving economy?
3. What are some of the groups that this viewpoint selects as positive examples of charitable giving, and what do you think makes them different?

Do Americans Give More to Charities When More People Are in Need?

No. Overall, for the last 64 years total giving has grown at an average annual rate of 3.3% adjusted for inflation. But the picture changes if you compare what's happened when the economy has grown versus when it has contracted. During years with economic growth, average giving has increased by 4.7%. During the years marked by economic downturns, average giving has actually decreased by 0.5%.

During economic downturns, more people are out of work and need a hand. But individuals, along with other sources of philanthropy including foundations, typically are making less income and have reduced wealth available, and so they decrease their giving accordingly.

The Great Recession was an extreme example. Total giving dropped by 7.2% in 2008, and then decreased by another 8% in 2009.

The change wasn't just because Americans had less money. Measuring giving as a share of gross domestic product—the total of all economic activity—is one way experts like us measure relative generosity on a national scale. U.S. giving as a percentage of GDP declined from 2.2% in 2007 to 2% in 2009.

Why Don't People Give More During Downturns?

There's a strong relationship between how much money Americans give to charity and their after-tax income. There is a similar correlation between giving and the stock market's performance. That means people give more when they feel that they have money to spare.

To be sure, some people see charity as a religious or moral obligation that they must try to uphold regardless of their personal economic circumstances. But for some of us, giving is a luxury rather than a necessity that can go on hold when times get tough.

At the same time, there's some evidence that people may try to help others deal with the hardships that recessions bring about. In 2008 and 2009, giving fell by a total of 15%. But giving to nonprofits such as food banks and homeless shelters that provide essential social services grew by 10%.

What About Foundations?

Foundations exist to fund charitable activities such as the pursuit of science, education, culture and religion. They are required by law to disburse at least 5% of their assets. There is no legal limit to how much they can spend, but in practice they try to retain most of their holdings to ensure that they can continue to exist in the long term.

And although spending more than 5% of their assets when times are tough might make a difference and is perfectly legal, historically, most have not taken this step.

We have tried to assess the validity of the concerns foundations have about spending more than 5% of their holdings every year by running thousands of simulations. These experiments modeled a variety of economic circumstances, different investment strategies, and various levels of disbursement relative to a foundation's total holdings.

We consistently determined that U.S. foundations would have enough funding to keep operating in the long term. That was true even if they were to distribute as much as 9% of their assets annually for 50 years or even a century.

However, it's important to acknowledge that their asset base would decline conspicuously. For example, unless they obtained additional capital and depending on how they manage their investments, foundations would lose between a third and a half of their starting value with a 7% payout rate.

Does It Have to Be That Way?

Fortunately, a growing group of foundations is rapidly responding to the many competing needs arising because of the pandemic. More than 40, so far, have joined forces to declare that they're making grants with fewer or no strings attached and quickly chipping in to support emergency-response funds in hard-hit communities.

The Bill and Melinda Gates Foundation, in particular, has committed US$125 million to speed up research into vaccines and treatments, along with everything it will take to swiftly distribute any breakthrough products as quickly as possible.

Likewise, the Chan Zuckerberg Initiative is partnering with the University of California, San Francisco and Stanford University to quadruple their testing and diagnosis capacity for the new coronavirus. They are also making a new dataset around the virus open access and machine-readable.

Regardless of how large philanthropic institutions respond to the repercussions from bringing the global economy to a screeching halt, it's important to keep in mind that while foundations play an important role in society, their impact is inherently limited.

All foundations combined held nearly $1 trillion in assets at the end of 2019, prior to the financial upheaval that has surely reduced the value of their holdings.

There's no amount they can give away over the coming years that would compare to the proposed federal stimulus package. It may top $2 trillion and is likely just the first salvo in response to this battle to stop the new coronavirus and its health and economic effects.

*"Foundations appear to be spending a
lot on influence."*

Corporations Give to Charities
for Self-Interested Reasons

Brian Wallheimer

*In this viewpoint, Brian Wallheimer makes the point that charitable
foundations may have less-than-charitable intentions when they
move around the money of their wealthy funders. In fact, this
viewpoint charges, these foundations can often operate as tools for
moving money from the hands of the wealthy into the hands of the
politically powerful in ways that are often too opaque to be registered
by ethics watchdogs. According to one count, companies spend almost
three times as much money on "politically motivated" charities than
directly through PACs, which can be more easily monitored and
disclosed. In this way, the charitable group can become a mechanism
for the creation of a less democratic society. Brian Wallheimer is a
journalist who has covered everything from the Illinois government
to casinos.*

As you read, consider the following questions:

1. Why do companies spend almost three times the amount on
   politically motivated charitable giving than they spend
   trying to influence politicians through PACs?

"How Corporations Use Charitable Giving to Wield Political Influence," by Brian
Wallheimer, Chicago Booth Review, June 7, 2018. Reprinted by permission.

2. What are some of the ways that this viewpoint says that voters suffer from this kind of power?
3. What makes Wallheimer conclude that taxpayers are essentially subsidizing the politics of special interests?

The hundreds of millions of dollars that US corporations give through political action committees have long raised red flags about special interests buying influence over elected officials. But research suggests that companies hand out even more money through charitable foundations to curry favor with lawmakers.

Companies spend almost three times the amount on politically motivated charitable giving than they spend trying to influence politicians through PACs, according to Chicago Booth's Marianne Bertrand, University of British Columbia's Matilde Bombardini and Francesco Trebbi, and Boston University's Raymond Fisman—and the amount is almost half as large as their federal lobbying spending. "Our analysis suggests that firms deploy their charitable foundations as a form of tax-exempt influence seeking," they write.

Companies have historically set up PACs to raise money to direct at campaigns and politicians. They've been around since 1944, when the Congress of Industrial Organizers formed one to help reelect President Franklin D. Roosevelt.

But companies also have charitable foundations, through which they fund philanthropic efforts. These efforts can help the for-profit side by burnishing the company's reputation and showcasing its socially responsible activities. Moreover, companies get tax breaks for donating to foundations.

Laws exist to trace the influence of companies and other special interests in politics, but researchers attempting to track and measure this influence have grown concerned about dark money, shadow lobbying, and other covert forms of influence—which apparently includes corporate philanthropy.

When a congressional representative obtained a seat on a committee important to the company, corporate foundations gave more to charities in that congressional district.

To explore this channel, Bertrand, Bombardini, Fisman, and Trebbi analyzed tax returns of 320 foundations affiliated with Fortune 500 and S&P 500 companies from 1998 to 2015, covering the 105th to the 114th US Congresses. The researchers correlated the foundations' charitable-giving patterns with congressional districts and committee assignments for members of Congress from the same period. They also used lobbying disclosure forms to identify issues important to companies.

The findings demonstrate that corporations increased giving to PACs that supported politicians who sat on congressional committees linked to the corporations' interests. A power-generation company was likely to fund a PAC supporting a lawmaker who sat on an energy committee, for example.

And they suggest that corporate foundation giving bore striking similarities to PAC behavior.

When a congressional representative obtained a seat on a committee important to the company, corporate foundations gave more to charities in that congressional district. When a representative left Congress, there was a decline in charitable giving in that district. When a replacement representative gained seniority over time, corporate foundations were again more generous in that district.

The researchers, by considering turnover in committee membership and issues relevant to companies, rule out the possibility that companies were simply donating to like-minded representatives or had nonpolitical interests in mind. Rather, they write that the activity of charitable foundations mimics patterns in PAC spending.

The foundations also gave more to charities that had a politician on the board. A nonprofit was four times more likely to receive grants from a corporate foundation when a politician sat on its board, according to the data. And a foundation was more likely to give to a nonprofit with a politician on the board if that politician was on a relevant congressional committee.

Why Capitalism Is Morally Superior

Nobel Laureate Edmund Phelps keys in on the economic and moral importance of "man the innovator." Corporatism is the economic system—or as Phelps says, a "set of economic institutions and an economic culture"—favored by Continental European countries, which he contrasts with the American model.

To paint with a broad brush . . . there are two economic systems in the West, both founded on private ownership. The first system is characterized by great openness to the implementation of new commercial ideas coming from people in private business, and by a great pluralism of views among the wealth-owners and financiers who decide which ideas to nurture by providing them the capital and incentives necessary for their development. Although much innovation comes from established companies, as in pharmaceuticals, much also comes from start-ups—particularly the most novel innovations. This is "free enterprise," also know as "capitalism."

The second private-ownership system has been modified by introducing institutions aimed at protecting the interests of "stakeholders" and "social partners." The system's institutions include most or all . . . of the massive components of the corporatist system of interwar Italy: big employer confederations, big unions, and monopolistic banks. Since the Second World War, a great deal of liberalization has taken place, no doubt. But new corporatist institutions have sprung up.

"Phelps: The Moral Superiority of Dynamic Capitalism," by Jay Richards, American Enterprise Institute, May 3, 2010.

Foundations appear to be spending a lot on influence. In 2014, there were $18 billion in total corporate charitable contributions, the researchers report. They estimate that 7 percent of that corporate charity, or $1.3 billion, was politically motivated. That amount is 280 percent higher than PAC contributions made that year, and represents 40 percent of the $3 billion in total companies spent on lobbying.

Because companies receive tax breaks for their charitable giving, taxpayers are essentially subsidizing the politics of special interests.

Politically minded foundation giving is, the researchers suggest, problematic. It can lead to less-than-optimal policies for voters, and because it's opaque, voters can't monitor or take into account information passing through back channels. Shareholders can't monitor it either, to make sure the giving serves their interests. And it may lead politically connected charities to be funded rather than more-efficient ones.

Moreover, because companies receive tax breaks for their charitable giving, taxpayers are essentially subsidizing the politics of special interests. "Unlike lobbying or campaign contributions, charitable giving potentially represents a tax-advantaged and hard-to-trace form of influence," write the researchers.

They note that while their data is from the United States, the phenomenon is global. They cite Israel's Holyland affair, where a real-estate developer donated to a charity founded by former Jerusalem mayor Uri Lupolianski.

"Given the lack of formal electoral or regulatory disclosure requirements, charitable giving may be a form of political influence that goes mostly undetected by voters and shareholders, and which is directly subsidized by taxpayers," write the researchers.

But the researchers sound a note of caution about crackdowns on money in politics: attempts to limit the influence of companies that are lobbying or giving through PACs could merely send the influence peddling to channels harder to see and document.

> "The Microsoft co-founder is a huge name in the tech world, but he and his wife also play a pivotal role in global health campaigns."

Bill and Melinda Gates Fight Infectious Diseases Through Their Charitable Foundation

The BBC

This viewpoint from the BBC reports on the Bill and Melinda Gates Foundation and focuses on the foundation's history since it was established by the titular pair of billionaires in 2000, a merger of two different, independent charitable endeavors. But money to support one of the modern world's most ubiquitous charities doesn't just come from the Microsoft fortune, it also comes from the fortunes of other rich people too. Currently, that money has made the organization into the largest private donor to the World Health Organization, second only to the money that goes to the UN health group from the U.S., which has turned Gates himself into a powerful public advocate for science-based medicine during the COVID-19 pandemic. The BBC is a government-owned news organization based in the UK.

"Bill and Melinda Gates Foundation: What is it and what does it do?" BBC, May 4, 2021. Reprinted by permission.

As you read, consider the following questions:

1. What is the pivotal role in global health campaigns that the Bill & Melinda Gates Foundation plays?
2. Where does the foundation get its money?
3. What are some of the ethical concerns that have been leveled about the foundation's work?

News that billionaires Bill and Melinda Gates are to separate after 27 years of marriage has sparked speculation over what will happen to their charitable foundation.

The Microsoft co-founder is a huge name in the tech world, but he and his wife also play a pivotal role in global health campaigns.

The Bill & Melinda Gates Foundation—the largest private body of its kind—spends billions of dollars every year on initiatives aimed at eradicating infectious diseases and reducing poverty.

How Did Their Foundation Start?

The Gates foundation was born in 2000 as a merger of two previous charitable endeavours.

The couple say they were inspired to do more by a newspaper report about how millions of children died of preventable diseases every year in poorer countries.

They said as new parents, the reports hit hard. They recalled sending the article to Bill's father with a note saying: "Dad, maybe we can do something about this."

"Those eight words changed the rest of our lives," the couple say on their foundation's website.

Bill gradually distanced himself from Microsoft to focus on the charity's work. Melinda, in her co-chair position, helped shape the organisation's direction with a particular interest in empowering women and girls.

What Does the Foundation Do?

Some of its earliest actions included pledges to the Global Fund organisation, which works to eradicate life-threatening diseases such as Malaria and Aids.

The Gates foundation was also a founding partner of Gavi, the Vaccine Alliance, created in 2000 to improve immunisation access in poor countries. It has donated more than $4bn to Gavi, which is currently the key player in distributing Covid vaccines in developing countries.

Improving sanitation has became another of the foundation's focuses. Bill Gates has done everything from brandishing a jar of poo on stage to drinking water from distilled faeces, in a bid to reduce stigma and showcase technological advances.

The foundation also does work in the US and says it has funded 20,000 university scholarships for high-achieving, low-income students of colour.

Headquartered in Seattle, the foundation has paid $54.8bn in grants to initiatives in 135 international countries.

The endeavour now has more than 1,600 employees in offices around the world—including in Delhi, Beijing and Johannesburg.

Where Does It Get Its Money From?

The Gates Foundation is the largest organisation of its kind in the world with an endowment of about $50bn (£36bn)—more than the GDP of some countries.

According to the foundation's website, the couple donated more than $36bn (£26bn) of their own wealth to it from 1994 to 2018.

Another major contributor is US tycoon Warren Buffett, who in 2006 made a lifetime pledge worth more than $30bn to the foundation.

Together with the investor, the couple launched the Giving Pledge campaign in 2010—encouraging other rich people to donate the majority of their wealth to good causes.

Does Everyone Agree with Its Work?

Although the foundation has done good work with its spending across the world, some have raised concerns about the ethics of a private endeavour wielding such great influence.

The foundation is the largest private donor to the World Health Organization (WHO), second only to the US with its annual donation in 2018. Concerns about this became more pointed after former President Donald Trump threatened to pull US funding.

Bill Gates has become a powerful public advocate for science-based medicine during the pandemic. This has shone new light on his involvement in global health and initiatives such as the Coalition for Epidemic Preparedness Innovations.

Will the Gates Foundation Continue Its Work?

In the statement announcing their divorce, the couple said they would "continue our work together at the foundation" in spite of the separation.

A spokesman for the foundation said they would remain co-chairs and trustees.

David Callahan, founder and editor of news website *Inside Philanthropy*, told the BBC's World Service that he expected the foundation's work to carry on.

"This is not some small family foundation that's going to fall apart because a marriage is falling apart, this is a large, professional institution," he said.

"They have built this from the ground up, over the last 20 years, they share a deep commitment to it, it's unlikely that either one of them would be happy to see it not continue to do the work that it does."

> "Free market capitalism is a mundane
> moral construct but any attempt
> to equate market conduct with
> a commonly held perception of
> morality can become tangled in
> normative discourse."

What If Capitalism Is Actually Moral?

Mikko Arevuo

In this viewpoint, Mikko Arevuo responds to moral criticisms of capitalism by suggesting that the problem is actually that people are using the wrong moral calculations. Pointing to ideas about morality that Arevuo found in a 2011 academic article called "Markets and Morality," he says that the moral value of market capitalism can be found through an idea called "mundane morality." According to Arevuo, mundane, market capitalism is morally good because the system creates an environment where people are able to pursue self-interest through "non-discriminatory impersonal exchanges governed by prices and free from normative interference." Arevuo is a senior lecturer on the subject of strategic management at the Cranfield School of Management in Bedfordshire, UK.

"Free Market Capitalism and Morality," by Mikko Arevuo, Institute of Economic Affairs, May 21, 2015. Reprinted by permission.

As you read, consider the following questions:

1. What does Arevou mean by giving "capitalism a human face?"
2. How is "outcome-based morality" different from regular morality?
3. What is Adam Smith's famous invisible hand?

I t has become increasingly difficult to make a case for the morality of markets even though free market capitalism has been unequalled in reducing poverty and discrimination, and in creating opportunities for social and economic advancement. The left has hijacked the moral high ground because the proponents of free markets have been incapable of mounting a credible defence for the benefits that free markets provide at both individual and societal levels. The recent financial crisis and the various market-rigging scandals have compounded the commonly held view that market behaviour is inherently immoral and divisive, even if it produces desirable outcomes. Public opinion has become dominated by an anti-market narrative that has led into increasingly aggressive calls for markets to be subjected to strict supervision and regulation to ensure 'moral behaviour' by market participants. The idea that free market capitalism is a mechanism to advance social order and decent humane relationships is considered outlandish.

Faced with hostile anti-market polemic, many policy makers and commentators seem to think that the answer is to give capitalism a *human face* by attaching adjectives such as "caring," "compassionate," or "responsible" to it. In reality, any attempts to modify the functioning of free markets through policy interventions and mould them into some *ideal* normative model invariably result in suboptimal outcomes compared to a market left to its own devices.

The root cause of the problem that free market capitalism faces is that modern society tries to assess the functioning of markets by attributes that are used to evaluate the morality of individual behaviour. In order to think about the morality of markets, or lack thereof, we need to consider morality as a two-dimensional construct. The first dimension of morality can be defined by the commonly held conception of "duty." The second dimension is concerned with outcome-based morality, e.g. behaving in a way that produces the best outcomes, including economic outcomes. Clark and Lee define these two sides of morality as *magnanimous morality* and *mundane morality* respectively.

Magnanimous morality is present in behaviours that help others in ways that is intentional, doing so at the benefactor's personal sacrifice, and providing help to identifiable beneficiaries. Magnanimous morality was strongly present in Adam Smith's writings as *positive merit* and he considered it an important part of human psyche: *"How selfish soever man may be supposed, there are evidently some principles in his nature, which interest him in the fortune of others, and render their happiness necessary to him, though he derives nothing from it except the pleasure of seeing it."*[1] This type of morality is selfless and highly personal between the benefactor and the beneficiary. In contrast, *mundane morality* can be considered broadly as obeying the generally accepted rules or norms of conduct such as telling the truth, honouring one's promises and contractual obligations, respecting the property rights of others, and refraining from intentionally harming others. Mundane morality is closely associated with Adam Smith's concept of *negative virtue* or justice that hinders us from hurting our neighbour, his property, or reputation.

Magnanimous morality refers to behaviour that most people associate with *true* moral conduct. It is deeply rooted in the Judeo-Christian value system illustrated by the biblical story of a widow dropping a few coins in a collection box, and Jesus telling his disciples: *"Verily I say to you, That this poor widow hath cast more in, than all they which have cast into the treasury; For all they did cast in of their abundance; but she of her want did cast in all that she had, even all her living."*[2] In the story, the widow acts intentionally at a great personal sacrifice without expecting anything in return for her actions. Although magnanimous morality may represent the highest virtue, it has problems in the wider economic context because such selfless altruistic behaviour is by necessity limited to a small group of benefactors and beneficiaries.

As the benefactor is not expected to earn a return from his good deeds, and because the beneficiaries are supposed to be known to the benefactors, these acts of kindness can probably be found in small homogenous communities that tend share a similar ethnic or religious background or worldview. Indeed, it can be argued that since magnanimous morality may foster the emergence of tightly knit, even closed social groups, it can become an isolating and divisive force within wider society. Moreover, as the benefactor is not expected to earn a return from good deeds, the long-term sustainability of magnanimous charity is limited by the benefactors' resource scarcity.

However, the concept of magnanimous morality has a strong hold on how we judge behaviour and it is incorrectly applied to judge the functioning of markets. Markets cannot operate under the conditions of magnanimous morality. They are mostly characterised by *negative virtue* or mundane morality.

An entrepreneur may make a significant impact in improving countless people's lives globally, far beyond what would be possible through the practice of selfless charity. But as the benefit to the wider society is tied to the entrepreneur's profit motive, his actions often do not warrant the same level of acceptance in the eyes of the society than selfless altruism. It is the profit motive, regardless of the positive market outcomes, that causes the critics to condemn market-mediated activity as selfish and immoral. Many critics point to a passage by Adam Smith that states that people are governed by self-interest: *"Every man is, no doubt, by nature, first and principally recommended to his own care; and as he is fitter to take care of himself than any other person, it is fit and right that it should be so."*[3] This narrow reading of Adam Smith ignores his insistence that although people are self-interested we nevertheless have to rely on the help of a vast network of people for every one of us to pursue our own well-being. Smith stated that in a civilized society we need the cooperation and assistance of others, and for each individual to direct his effort where:

> "*its produce may be of the greatest value; every individual necessarily labours to render the annual revenue of society as great as he can. He generally, indeed, neither intends to promote the public interest, nor knows how much he is promoting it [...] By pursuing his own interest he frequently promotes that of the society more effectually than when he really intends to promote it.*"[4]

Adam Smith's famous "invisible hand" is a manifestation of mundane moral conduct. It does not involve the conditions of magnanimous morality of intention, personal sacrifice, or identifiable beneficiaries. However, as Clark and Lee point out, the invisible hand provides more help because people do not intend to provide it. Help is motivated and accompanied by personal gain and the benefits accrue to society as a whole, rather than to an easily identifiable group of people. Therefore, markets do not require behaviour that is seen as moral to produce positive outcomes. The market may be indifferent to morality, but since it aligns self-interested behavior with satisfying the needs of others, it delivers positive outcomes to the wider society as long as markets are governed by Smithian negative virtue of lawful conduct.

Free market capitalism is a mundane moral construct but any attempt to equate market conduct with a commonly held perception of morality can become tangled in normative discourse. A more productive approach to address the critics of free markets is to focus on the positive outcomes of free markets that have moral merit in them on both national and global scale. In terms of policy debate, free market advocates should seek to influence decision-makers to create an environment where markets can operate free from political and special interest group interference. *The Economist* (2010:16) highlighted attempts in European countries to maintain and promote social cohesion with greater government control over the economy and concluded "*that many of the policies espoused in the name of social cohesion do not promote compassion over cruelty. Rather, they encourage decline, entrench divisions, and thus threaten the harmony they pretend to nurture.*" The mundane morality of the invisible hand creates an environment where each one of us is able to pursue our own self-interest through non-discriminatory impersonal exchanges governed by prices and free from normative interference. It is this mechanism that allows us to realize the morally virtuous outcomes of prosperity, reduced poverty and discrimination.

References

[1] Adam Smith, *The Theory of Moral Sentiments,* Part I, Section I, Chapter I, 1 [1759], (Cambridge Texts in the History of Philosophy, Knut Haakonssen, Ed., 2009).

[2] St. Mark 14:18-9, King James Version of The Bible, Standard Text Edition, Cambridge University Press.

[3] Adam Smith, *The Theory of Moral Sentiments,* [1759], (Cambridge Texts in the History of Philosophy, Knut Haakonssen, Ed., 2009).

[4] Adam Smith, *The Wealth of Nations* [1776], Penguin Classics, 1999.

> "Philanthropy Roundtable celebrates this continued generosity to U.S. charities, which is vital for our free society and improves people's lives, while recognizing that inflation and market conditions may impact charitable giving in future years."

Despite an Increase in Giving, Charity Can't Keep Pace with Inflation

Esther Larson

In this viewpoint, Esther Larson shows how charitable giving increased in the U.S. in response to the COVID-19 pandemic. Larson asserts that the pandemic, economic crisis, and racial justice concerns spurred Americans to give more to charities in 2020, a trend that continued in 2021. However, despite an increase in giving, nonprofits faced challenges because the rate of giving still could not keep up with the rate of inflation. While the increase in giving seems impressive— and according to Larson is still a testament to Americans' generosity and the importance of charitable giving—due to inflation, it had a smaller impact. Larson also considers trends in different areas of charitable giving. Esther Larson is a program director at Philanthropy Roundtable.

"Giving USA Report Shows 2021 Charitable Giving Strong, But Did Not Keep Pace with Inflation," by Esther Larson, Philanthropy Roundtable. Reprinted by permission.

As you read, consider the following questions:

1. According to this viewpoint, how did charitable giving in the U.S. in 2021 compare to giving in 2020?
2. What are mega gifts?
3. Of the different areas of giving discussed, which area is the only one that experienced a decline in giving?

Charitable giving in the United States remained strong in 2021, as Americans gave an estimated $484.85 billion to U.S. charities, according to *Giving USA 2022: The Annual Report on Philanthropy for the Year 2021*.

This marks a 4% increase in total charitable giving in 2021, following record-setting numbers in 2020, when Americans responded to the COVID-19 pandemic and economic turmoil by donating $466.23 billion to charity. However, while giving increased in current dollars, it remained flat (-0.7%) after adjusting for inflation. Philanthropy Roundtable celebrates this continued generosity to U.S. charities, which is vital for our free society and improves people's lives, while recognizing that inflation and market conditions may impact charitable giving in future years.

"The story of charitable giving in 2021 is closely tied to the events of 2020, a historic year that included a global pandemic, economic crisis and recovery, efforts to advance racial justice and an unprecedented philanthropic response," said Laura MacDonald, chair of Giving USA Foundation and principal and founder of Benefactor Group. "In 2021, Americans continued giving more generously than before the pandemic. However, the growth in giving did not keep pace with inflation, causing challenges for many nonprofits. In 2021, many donors returned to their favored causes, with many of the sectors that struggled in 2020 making a recovery in 2021."

With gifts by the country's largest donors, including MacKenzie Scott and Elon Musk, attracting global attention, the report reveals that mega gifts, defined as gifts of $450 million or more, reached a total of nearly $15 billion in 2021—representing about 5% of all individual giving last year. Though these mega gifts are significant, smaller scale philanthropy by individual Americans of all socioeconomic levels represented a significant 70% of total giving to U.S. charities.

Below are some highlights from the report, published by Giving USA Foundation and researched and written by the Indiana University Lilly Family School of Philanthropy at IUPUI:

- "Giving by individuals totaled an estimated $326.87 billion, rising 4.9% (staying flat at 0.2%, adjusted for inflation).[1]
- Giving by foundations grew 3.4%, to an estimated $90.88 billion (-1.2%, adjusted for inflation). Giving by foundations, which has grown in 10 of the last 11 years, represented 19% of total giving in 2021, its largest share on record. This year's giving is the second-highest dollar amount on record when adjusted for inflation.
- Giving to religion grew by 5.4% with an estimated $135.78 billion in contributions (flat at 0.7% adjusted for inflation)."
- Of note: Given the pandemic-related shutdowns and many religious communities unable to worship in person for periods throughout 2021, this increase (flat with inflation) giving pattern is worth noting. With recent reports showing stagnation and/or decline in religious participation across America, religious giving trends will continue to be important datapoints to track year over year as predictions are this giving may potentially be in decline.
- "Giving to human services increased by an estimated 2.2% totaling $65.33 billion (-2.4%, adjusted for inflation)."
- Of note: Though the stock market and GDP grew significantly in 2021, not all sectors in the economy experienced growth. Given employment concerns and ongoing pandemic related issues, this continued investment in human services marks the continued recognition of community needs by the funding community.

- "Giving to arts, culture and humanities is estimated to have increased 27.5% to $23.50 billion (21.8%, adjusted for inflation)."
- Of note: With emergency and crisis needs subsiding as the pandemic waned, rebound for funding to arts, culture and humanities is significant. As the U.S. and the world recover from the trauma and impact of the pandemic, funding for these areas will likely increase in scope and importance.
- "Giving to education is estimated to have declined 2.8% to $70.79 billion (-7.2% adjusted for inflation). Education giving includes contributions to K-12 schools, higher education and libraries."
- Of note: With increased scrutiny of schools, leadership and curriculum in recent years, this decline in funding to education is important. Contributing factors could include changes in higher education giving with alumni evolving their giving patterns due to donor intent and academic freedom concerns as well as trends such as micro-schooling, homeschooling and other innovations in education which may also have impacted education related funding.

Given the evolution of giving vehicles Americans use to support charity, this year's report includes a new chapter dedicated to understanding giving patterns of donor-advised funds and their donors. "Giving to public-society benefit organizations has grown in 11 of the last 12 years and is one of the few sectors that grew in both 2020 and 2021," said Patrick M. Rooney, Ph.D., executive associate dean for academic programs at the Lilly Family School of Philanthropy. "Growth in this subsector aligns with increased support for legal rights and voting nonprofits, but it is most strongly driven by giving to national donor-advised funds (DAFs). Some of America's wealthiest individuals have announced major gifts to national DAFs, and the growth in the stock market more generally in the past two years has helped to bolster this subsector."

Nevertheless, inflation and other economic conditions last year exerted pressure on the philanthropic sector. Una Osili, Ph.D., associate dean for research and international programs at the Lilly Family School of Philanthropy said, "While the stock market performed well in 2021, there were some economic factors that may have affected nonprofits' operations, such as labor shortages, supply chain interruptions and ongoing high demand for services. The growth that we see for most of the subsectors in 2021 is a reminder of the resilience and innovation that help to drive the philanthropic sector."

Indeed, as concerns about a potential recession continue to rise, we believe economic conditions could affect future charitable giving. Yet we also agree with Dr. Osili's assertion that "resilience and innovation ... help to drive the philanthropic sector." We look forward to continuing to witness the generous American spirit that helps uplift communities throughout our country and world.

> *"Unfortunately, the singular focus on diversity doesn't recognize an equitable redistribution of resources and an inclusionary workplace as important goals and values."*

Corporations Support Diversity Initiatives, but Not in a Way that Benefits Society

Aryan Karimi

In this viewpoint, Aryan Karimi takes a different approach to the question of the morality of capitalism by considering the moral values of equity, diversity, and inclusion (EDI) policies in corporations. It has become increasingly common for the amount of diversity within a company or industry to be measured and made public. These conversations were intended to help corporations and industries shed prejudices, but instead they have simply encouraged them to adopt "diversity" as a value in a strictly superficial way that does not actually give voice to the marginalized people they hire. Additionally, Karimi argues that the values of equity and inclusion rarely actually factor into these conversations. Corporations simply use diversity statistics for status, not to have a positive impact on society. Aryan Karimi is an assistant professor of sociology at the University of British Columbia.

"How Equity, Diversity and Inclusion Policies Are Becoming a Tool for Capitalism," by Aryan Karimi, The Conversation, December 22, 2022. https://theconversation.com/how-equity-diversity-and-inclusion-policies-are-becoming-a-tool-for-capitalism-196534. Licensed under CC BY-ND 4.0 International.

As you read, consider the following questions:

1. Did Karimi at one point believe that EDI policies could help industries become more ethical?
2. What are "pretendians" and how do they factor into the discussion of EDI policies in this viewpoint?
3. How do corporate diversity initiatives cause marginalized individuals to lose their voice, according to Karimi?

In capitalistic economies like those in the West, wealth and status accumulation often drive our every endeavour.

Education, skills training and social networks, among other aspects, become tools that we use in this rat race to push ahead for our interests.

Such questionable ethics seem ripe for a reassessment.

I once believed equity, diversity and inclusion (EDI) policies for government and industry could help.

In 2016, while at the University of Alberta's Office of Employment Equity, I co-authored a preliminary Equity, Diversity, and Inclusion (EDI) Educational Framework. At the time, my understanding was that EDI policies were primarily a set of tools that we could use to have conversations about individual stories and backgrounds, unconscious biases and our common traits as human beings.

As such, EDI conversations would mean that people could share their concerns and shed prejudices; they could feel that they were being seen and heard for who they are.

My goal was to implement EDI policies to prepare future generations for "democratic citizenship." Increasingly, however, I am seeing a 180-degree shift in how EDI is understood and used at individual and institutional levels.

Three Components of EDI

Recent employment data on public service employees and large higher-education institutions across Canada show a remarkably diverse workforce. This is an admirable achievement. But diversity shouldn't be mistaken for equity and inclusion.

The *equity* component of EDI policies emphasizes the need to lift up individuals. They require an equitable redistribution of institutional resources. The *inclusion* component calls for conversations to help us learn about different ways of life.

The problem is that in our capitalist economy, equity and inclusion have been sidelined. Instead, diversity — involving characteristics that include gender, race and sexual orientation — has become yet another tool to accumulate resources and social status.

Take the case of contested identity claims, the "pretendians" who claim to be of Indigenous heritage. In Canada and the United States, pretendians can leverage EDI policies and abuse their supposed Indigenous status to gain employment and financial resources or capital.

Meantime, Indigenous people — many of whom don't have basic resources to begin with — are left behind, if not intentionally kept back by the state and various institutions.

In both public and private sectors, EDI policies are seemingly falling short of creating an inclusionary workplace. Instead of providing institution-wide opportunities for dialogue among employees to create inclusionary spaces, institutions now see the diversity component of EDI as a means of ticking boxes and improving their institutional status.

Diversity Becomes a Ranking Tool

For example, in the case of universities, it used to be common to count the total numbers of publications and professor-student ratio to rank them. Now diversity has become an additional metric.

This means that universities are motivated to hire from marginalized groups. This helps the institutions climb in the ranks, attracts more students who might be mindful of diversity and ultimately makes the university eligible to receive larger financial grants and donations.

Again, diversity has not necessarily meant a more equitable campus community, although some certainly pursue this goal. The newly hired members of the marginalized groups often remain on the margins of these institutions.

These individuals — token representations of diversity — help enhance the institutions' rankings while losing their own voice and identity to the very same institutions. Their politics, stories and self-expression have to either fade into the institutionalized way of life at their workplace, or, to survive, they must learn not to challenge the dominant traditions.

Diversity, but No Equity or Inclusion

EDI initiatives now seem to be focused primarily on diversity without equity and inclusion. And diversity has become a metric of assessing achievements and rankings. It's no surprise that individuals and institutions like universities might use diversity to compete for resources and status.

Unfortunately, the singular focus on diversity doesn't recognize an equitable redistribution of resources and an inclusionary workplace as important goals and values.

Research shows that diversity without effective communication and collaboration across groups results in "silo" scenarios. Power struggles increase as individuals team up as group members and categorize others as outsiders who must be kept from accessing resources.

Using diversity for status and financial benefit is the antithesis of EDI as a tool for democratic and equitable citizenship where all voices are heard and supported. There must be a better way to promote EDI without falling into the capitalistic trap of competitions for resources and status.

Periodical and Internet Sources Bibliography

The following articles have been selected to supplement the diverse views presented in this chapter.

Ericka Andersen, "America's Coming Charity Deficit," *Wall Street Journal*, June 30, 2022. https://www.wsj.com/articles/americas-charity-deficit-giving-nones-generosity-crisis-baby-boomers-faith-religion-families-civil-society-11656618437.

Peter Coy, "The Thorny Questions Raised by Charitable Giving," *New York Times*, December 26, 2022. https://www.nytimes.com/2022/12/26/opinion/philanthropy-charitable-giving-holiday.html.

Charles Duhigg, "How Venture Capitalists Are Deforming Capitalism," *New Yorker*, November 30, 2020. https://www.newyorker.com/magazine/2020/11/30/how-venture-capitalists-are-deforming-capitalism.

Nick French, "How Analytic Philosophers Have Made Sense of Capitalism," *Jacobin,* January 25, 2023. https://jacobin.com/2023/01/analytic-philosophy-marxism-capitalism-moral-individualism.

Anand Giridharadas, "This Week, Billionaires Made a Strong Case for Abolishing Themselves," *New York Times*, November 19, 2022. https://www.nytimes.com/2022/11/19/opinion/musk-trump-bezos-bankman-fried-billionaires.html.

Nathan Heller, "The Philosopher Redefining Equality," *New Yorker*, December 31, 2018. https://www.newyorker.com/magazine/2019/01/07/the-philosopher-redefining-equality.

Andy Kessler, "'Effective Altruism' Is Neither," *Wall Street Journal*, July 24, 2022. https://www.wsj.com/articles/effective-altruism-is-neither-bankman-fried-givewell-philanthropy-taxes-capitalism-artificial-intelligence-pandemic-pet-projects-11658658039.

Michael Novak, "Capitalism Is the Most Moral of a Bad Lot of Economic Systems," *New York Times*, March 23, 2015. https://www.nytimes.com/roomfordebate/2014/06/25/has-capitalism-become-incompatible-with-christianity/capitalism-is-the-most-moral-of-a-bad-lot-of-economic-systems.

Naomi Schaefer Riley, "The Woke Threat to Philanthropy," *Wall Street Journal*, July 16, 2021. https://www.wsj.com/articles/elise-westhoff-woke-philanthropy-cancel-culture-charity-11626448092.

John Stossel, "Private Charity Beats One-Size-Fits-All Government," *Reason*, December 2, 2020. https://reason.com/2020/12/02/private-charity-beats-one-size-fits-all-government.

Adrian Wooldridge, "America's Work Ethic Is Under Assault," *Bloomberg*, January 31, 2023. https://www.washingtonpost.com/business/americas-work-ethic-is-under-assault/2023/01/31/d26de368-a129-11ed-8b47-9863fda8e494_story.html.

For Further Discussion

Chapter 1

1. Based on the viewpoints you read in this chapter, how does the popularity of something like the gig economy impact the larger popularity of capitalism?
2. Do you think capitalism can fight climate change? Use examples from the viewpoints in this chapter to explain your answer.
3. Has Noel Castree changed how you think about the word "crisis?" Why or why not?

Chapter 2

1. Based on the viewpoints in this chapter, why do you think socialists have a different idea of how long capitalism has existed?
2. Do new technologies change anything fundamental about capitalism? Why or why not?
3. Why do you think that an idea like "bartering" appealed to Gillian Tett, based on her viewpoint?

Chapter 3

1. What was the overall legacy of the collapse of the Soviet Union on the prospect of finding alternatives to capitalism?
2. According to the viewpoint by Victoria Méndez, are mutual aid groups new? If not, what are some early examples of them?
3. After reading the viewpoint in this chapter by Samuel Arnold, do you think there is a major distinction between socialism and democratic socialism? Why or why not?

Chapter 4

1. Based on what you have read in the viewpoints in this chapter, how does charitable giving change the moral argument for or against capitalism?
2. What are some of the big needs that charities generally try to fill, based on what you have read?
3. According to the viewpoints in this chapter, what are some reasons for being suspicious of charitable organizations?

Organizations to Contact

The editors have compiled the following list of organizations concerned with the issues debated in this book. The descriptions are derived from materials provided by the organizations. All have publications or information available for interested readers. The list was compiled on the date of publication of the present volume; the information provided here may change. Be aware that many organizations take several weeks or longer to respond to inquiries, so allow as much time as possible.

Adam Smith Institute

23 Great Smith Street
London SW1P 3DJ
United Kingdom
02072224995
email: info@adamsmith.org
website: www.adamsmith.org

Not directly connected to the influential pro-free market economist Adam Smith, the Adam Smith Institute is considered a "pioneer of privatisation" in politics in the UK. Over the past few years, the group has supported programs like reforming the tax system, as well as efforts to privatize railways and increase immigration.

American Enterprise Institute (AEI)

1789 Massachusetts Avenue, NW
Washington, DC 20036
(202) 862-5800
email: MediaServices@aei.org
website: www.aei.org

Started in 1938, the American Enterprise Institute was established by the American industrialist Lewis H. Brown. According to its mission statement, the group seeks to generate greater public knowledge and understanding of the social and economic advantages accruing to the American people through the maintenance of the system of free, competitive enterprise.

Brookings Institution

1775 Massachusetts Ave., NW
Washington, DC 20036
(202) 797-6000
email: media@brookings.edu
website: www.brookings.edu

One of the older think tanks that promote capitalism, the Brookings Institution dates to 1916 and was started by Robert S. Brookings, who once ran a company that dominated the woodenware trade. According to its website, Brookings supports human-centered capitalism. These days, the organization's biggest funders are the are foundations like the Bill & Melinda Gates Foundation, the William and Flora Hewlett Foundation, the Hutchins Family Foundation, as well as large banks like JPMorgan Chase.

Cato Institute

1000 Massachusetts Ave. NW
Washington, DC 20001
(202) 842-0200
website: www.cato.org

A libertarian, pro-capitalist think tank that has operated since 1977, the Cato Institute was named after a series of letters authored between 1720 and 1723 by the British writers John Trenchard and Thomas Gordon, and was co-founded by Charles Koch, the industrialist behind Koch Industries. These days, the Cato Institute is a central force for promoting policy that supports free market capitalism.

Democratic Socialists of America

PO Box 1038
New York, NY 10272
(212) 727-8610
email: media@dsausa.org
website: www.dsausa.org

One of the leading political groups that identify themselves as opposed to capitalism is the Democratic Socialists of America, a political organization that started in 1982 as an offshoot of the now-defunct Socialist Party of America. On its website, the group defines capitalism as a system designed by the owning class to exploit the rest of us for their own profit, adding "we must replace it with democratic socialism." Over the past few years, the group has backed a number of successful political campaigns, like that of Congresswoman Alexandria Ocasio-Cortez.

Fraser Institute

4th Floor, 1770 Burrard Street
Vancouver BC
Canada V6J 3G7
(604) 688-0221
email: info@fraserinstitute.org
website: https://fraserinstitute.org

The Fraser Institute is widely known as one of the major pro-capitalist think tanks operating in Canadian politics and dates to 1974, when it was cofounded by a top executive at MacMillan Bloedel, a large forestry company. The organization argues that capitalism saved the world and has existed forever when not forcibly prevented by rulers. These days, the group is funded by the Koch brothers as well as companies like ExxonMobil.

Gravel Institute

(914) 295-2566
email: contact@gravelinstitute.org
website: https://gravelinstitute.org

A left-wing group founded by the late former Senator Mike Gravel, the Gravel Institute is a nonprofit that puts out videos and articles with names like "Does Capitalism Actually Reduce Poverty?" and "How Capitalism Exploits You." Its focus is on building progressive popular education and spreading progressive ideas to a new audience.

The Heritage Foundation

214 Massachusetts Ave. NE
Washington DC 20002
(800) 546-2843
email: info@heritage.org
website: www.heritage.org

A Washington, DC-based think tank that has operated since the 1970s, the Heritage Foundation became popular during the Reagan administration a decade later. According to its website, the group takes the position that capitalism benefits all, as seen by the lessening of historical racial and gender disparities. Since its start, the group has been financed by various capitalists, starting with its founder Joseph Coors, of the family that owns the Coors Brewing Company.

Hoover Institution on War, Revolution and Peace at Stanford University

434 Galvez Mall
Stanford University
Stanford, CA 94305
website: www.hoover.org

The Hoover Institution is a public policy think tank and research institution that supports ideas like the humane side of capitalism.

The group is funded by numerous other foundations as well as Stanford University, where former President Herbert Hoover had been among the school's first graduates.

People's Policy Project

email: staff@peoplespolicyproject.org
website: www.peoplespolicyproject.org

A think tank started by the American lawyer, blogger, and policy analyst Matt Bruenig, the People's Policy Project is an online think tank that aims to fill the holes left by the current think tank landscape with a special focus on socialist and social democratic economic ideas, according to its website. The kinds of ideas that this group has backed include extending tax credits and providing universal pregnancy coverage and parental leave.

Bibliography of Books

David Graeber. *Debt: The First 5000 Years*. New York, NY: Melville House, 2011.

Silvia Federici. *Beyond the Periphery of the Skin: Rethinking, Remaking, and Reclaiming the Body in Contemporary Capitalism*. Binghamton, NY: PM Press, 2020.

Rebecca Henderson. *Reimagining Capitalism in a World on Fire*. New York, NY: PublicAffairs, 2020.

Kimberly Kay Hoang. *Spiderweb Capitalism: How Global Elites Exploit Frontier Markets*. Princeton, NJ: Princeton University Press, 2022.

Amelia Horgan. *Lost in Work: Escaping Capitalism*. London, UK: Pluto Press, 2021.

Tansy E. Hoskins. *The Anti-Capitalist Book of Fashion*. London, UK: Pluto Press, 2022.

Avery Elizabeth Hurt, ed. *The Corporatization of America* (Opposing Viewpoints). Buffalo, NY: Greenhaven Publishing, 2023.

Eva Illouz. *Cold Intimacies: The Making of Emotional Capitalism*. Cambridge, UK: Polity, 2007.

Tim Jackson. *Post Growth: Life after Capitalism*. Cambridge, UK: Polity, 2021.

Andrew Karpan, ed. *White Collar Crime* (Opposing Viewpoints). Buffalo, NY: Greenhaven Publishing, 2023.

Naomi Klein. *This Changes Everything: Capitalism vs. The Climate*. New York, NY: Simon & Schuster, 2014.

Anna Lowenhaupt Tsing. *The Mushroom at the End of the World: On the Possibility of Life in Capitalist Ruins*. Princeton, NJ: Princeton University Press, 2021.

Mariana Mazzucato. *The Value of Everything: Making & Taking in the Global Economy*. New York, NY: PublicAffairs, 2020.

Ellen Meiksins Wood. *The Origin of Capitalism: A Longer View*. Brooklyn, NY: Verso, 2017.

Jason W. Moore. *Capitalism in the Web of Life: Ecology and the Accumulation of Capital*. Brooklyn, NY: Verso, 2015.

Thomas Piketty. *The Economics of Inequality*. Cambridge, MA: The Belknap Press: 2015.

Robert B. Reich. *The System: Who Rigged It, How We Fix It*. New York, NY: Vintage, 2021.

Hadas Thier. *A People's Guide to Capitalism: An Introduction to Marxist Economics*. Chicago, IL: Haymarket Books, 2020.

Rainer Zitelmann. *The Power of Capitalism: A Journey Through Recent History Across Five Continents*. London, UK: LID Publishing, 2019.

Index

X